Prayer for a multicultural church
INTRODUCTION

Signs of the times

In Miami, Haitian women clad in multicolored skirts and scarves gracefully dance up the aisle bearing the gifts in the offertory procession. In a small church in Indiantown, Florida, the marimba is the primary instrument in a congregation whose participants wear the indigenous dress of their Mayan ancestors and listen to the Gospel in Spanish and Kanjobal, their Mayan dialect. The lilting tones of songs in Tagalog, Chinese, and Vietnamese drift from churches in Los Angeles; and in Nebraska, Iraqi and Sudanese congregations gather to celebrate in their native tongues. Small farming communities in Iowa, mining communities in rural Appalachia, and retirement communities in Arizona gather together at the table of the Lord.

Drumbeats and dance, Spanish, Chinese, French, Vietnamese, Portuguese, English, colorful costumes and conservative suits, exotic instruments and the traditional organ, statues of St. Joseph and the Virgin of Guadalupe. This is the Catholic Church today—a Church of many faces and many languages; a Church of many cultures and varied life experiences; a Church of the wealthy and a Church of the marginalized. This is the Church that beckons us to move beyond ourselves and to touch the world around us with love and compassion.

Coming together as community is central to our worship, yet our diversity often makes it difficult for all to feel welcome. Our styles of worship, our expectations of the minister and of the community, and our differing ideas about the place of communal worship in our lives often prevent us from seeing our oneness. Recent advances in the field of education can provide us with new ways of looking at prayer and worship that invite all to "come as you are" to God's house.

The theory of multiple intelligences

In 1983 Dr. Howard Gardner of Harvard University published a book titled *Frames of Mind*[1] that forever changed the definition of *intelligence*. His breakthrough work, based on his own cross-cultural perspective of human cognition, posited that human beings do not have a single kind of intelligence but, rather, multiple intelligences. He defined an intelligence as:

- the capacity to solve problems that one encounters in real life.
- the ability to generate new problems to solve.
- the ability to make something or offer a service that is valued within one's culture.[2]

His work significantly impacts our understanding of intelligence across cultures. In his work he demonstrates that intelligence is partly based on the culture into which one is born and further defined by one's life experiences.

The eight intelligences

Gardner has thus far identified eight intelligences:

- The Verbal-Linguistic Intelligence is characterized by the ability to use words effectively and to enjoy reading, writing, speaking, and listening.
- The Logical-Mathematic Intelligence is characterized by the ability to use numbers effectively, the capacity to recognize patterns and relationships, and the skill to solve problems through logic.
- The Visual-Spatial Intelligence is characterized by the ability to create mental images and the capacity to use the visual arts in personal expression.
- The Bodily-Kinesthetic Intelligence involves physical coordination and dexterity and is characterized by well-developed gross and fine motor coordination skills.
- The Musical-Rhythmic Intelligence involves understanding and expressing oneself through music and the sensitivity to pitch, tone, and rhythm.
- The Naturalist Intelligence is characterized by sensitivity to the natural environment, the capacity to observe patterns in nature, and the ability to identify and classify natural and human-made systems.
- The Intrapersonal Intelligence is characterized by the capacity to understand one's inner motivations and feelings and the ability to control and direct them.
- The Interpersonal Intelligence is characterized by the capacity to interact with others as well as the ability to perceive and understand others' temperaments, moods, and feelings.

Although these eight intelligences have been validated against the criteria Gardner developed, he asserts that many more intelligences may exist. Precisely because of the role he sees culture play in developing intelligence, he points out that many cultures may develop the capacity to solve problems that are not familiar to us.

No one individual operates solely out of a single intelligence but, rather, uses unique combinations of all the intelligences. In any person, some of the intelligences are stronger than others; as a result, different people have different learning styles. Each intelligence uses its own pathway to the brain to enable an individual to take in, process, and give back information. Individual intelligence patterns are as unique as fingerprints.

Prayer and intelligence

The theory of multiple intelligences has revolutionized our understanding of how the human brain functions and has had a phenomenal impact on the field of education. However, this theory also has applications to prayer and worship. Instead of viewing the intelligences simply as pathways to the brain, they can also be indicative of pathways to God. Looking at the intelligences through the lens of prayer opens up a variety of prayer options and possibilities which can lead people into more meaningful forms of prayer and help dissolve language and cultural barriers.

Following the introduction is a Multiple Intelligences Prayer Inventory to help you determine your preferred style or styles of prayer. Note those styles that resonate with you, but also take time to try those that are not your preferred types. By doing so, you can develop your intelligences that are less developed as well as strengthen your prayer life by engaging in forms of prayer that seem more difficult.

Prayer is personal. When we pray by ourselves, we have the option of choosing the style that meets our individual needs at any given time. However, during communal worship, it is imperative that a variety of the intelligences be incorporated into liturgies and prayer services. It is equally as important to facilitate an understanding on the part of the community that when we come together as Church to pray and worship, we come as the people of God and that the desire to worship together is more important than our individual likes and dislikes. An understanding of the use of multiple intelligences can lead to an understanding of why different people express themselves differently in prayer and that there is no one best way to pray. The ultimate goal is to move beyond comments like "I don't like the music at the Mass," or "I think it's sinful for people to dance up the aisles," and to foster the realization that our prayer needs are as diverse as our personalities and that it is our desire to come together as community that unites us, not any single style of worship.

The remaining chapters of this book will look at each intelligence individually and suggest a variety of prayer options that will open new pathways to God. The insights gained through the study of multiple intelligences can lead to deeper and more meaningful prayer experiences individually and communally. Understanding that intelligence itself is partially a cultural phenomenon can lead to prayer and worship that invite people of all cultures and traditions to explore new ways of coming to know the God within, without, above, and around all of creation.

Each chapter will open with a short introduction about how prayer can be enhanced and deepened by approaching it through the particular intelligence. The introduction is followed by a variety of suggestions to tap into that intelligence. These suggestions are in no specific order, and each can be used individually or incorporated into communal worship. You will undoubtedly notice that each prayer option is not self-contained or mutually exclusive; rather, each one overlaps and touches more than one intelligence. Each prayer option, however, is placed in the chapter of the intelligence it relies most strongly upon.

This book is designed for personal use and as a resource for religious educators from preschool through adult levels, for RCIA leaders, liturgists, and pastoral associates, and for anyone else wishing to explore more deeply the many ways of knowing God in prayer.

---

[1] Gardner, Howard. *Frames of Minds*. Basic Books: HarperCollins, 1983.

[2] Campbell, Linda, Bruce Campbell & Dee Dickinson. *Teaching & Learning Through Multiple Intelligences*. Allyn & Bacon, 1999.

Multiple intelligences prayer inventory

A spiritual autobiography is the story of your relationship to God—the path from birth to where you are now. The following questions invite you to reflect and write about your personal spiritual journey.

Part I

Complete each section by placing a check mark next to each statement you feel accurately describes you. Leave blank any statements that do not describe you. Total the number of check marks in each section.

Section 1

_____ I enjoy spiritual reading.
_____ I enjoy keeping a journal.
_____ I express myself well with words, both written and oral.
_____ I memorize prayers easily.
_____ I like reading and writing poetry.
_____ I enjoy reading the psalms.
_____ I have a good memory for recalling stories.
_____ I enjoy listening to stories.
_____ I like to write my own prayers.
_____ I enjoy speaking in front of a group about things that are important to me.
_____ ***Total for Section 1***

Section 2

_____ I appreciate the fact that the Mass follows the same pattern, no matter where in the world it is being celebrated.
_____ I like to think about "what if" questions (example: What if Jesus came back today?).
_____ I am very organized.
_____ I like comparing the accounts of similar stories told by different Gospel writers.
_____ I have a regular prayer schedule.

_____ I keep a list of people I want to pray for and situations I want to pray about.

_____ I like meditation techniques that follow a prescribed pattern.

_____ Structure is important to me.

_____ I like clear, logical explanations for events.

_____ I like prayers that follow a specific pattern (i.e. the rosary).

_____ *Total for Section 2*

Section 3

_____ I enjoy prayer using guided imagery.

_____ Environment is important to my prayer life.

_____ I enjoy praying with pictures.

_____ I have a good imagination.

_____ I like to draw or doodle.

_____ I prefer to draw my ideas rather than write them down.

_____ I enjoy beautiful art in sacred places.

_____ I sometimes imagine myself having a conversation with Jesus or one of the Apostles.

_____ I can visualize the events in Bible stories.

_____ I often see clear images when I close my eyes.

_____ *Total for Section 3*

Section 4

_____ I like to sing.

_____ I play a musical instrument.

_____ Music is an important part of liturgy for me.

_____ I remember the words to songs easily.

_____ I frequently pray with music.

_____ I can easily keep time to a piece of music with a percussion instrument such as a tambourine, a drum, or maracas.

_____ I have a good sense of rhythm.

_____ Music affects me emotionally.

_____ I am or would like to be in a handbell choir.

_____ I enjoy chanting the psalms.

_____ *Total for Section 4*

Section 5

_____ I like to dance.
_____ I find it difficult to sit still for long periods of time.
_____ I enjoy doing dramatizations of Bible stories.
_____ My sense of balance and coordination are good.
_____ I enjoy liturgical dance/movement.
_____ I enjoy walking the labyrinth.
_____ I recognize the importance of the body, mind, spirit connection in prayer.
_____ I enjoy creating interpretive dances.
_____ I learn by doing.
_____ I pray better when I am walking or otherwise physically involved.
_____ ***Total for Section 5***

Section 6

_____ I enjoy observing the changes which take place in nature.
_____ I am actively involved in environmental issues.
_____ I pray better in nature.
_____ I enjoy outdoor activities.
_____ I enjoy nature walks.
_____ I often see patterns and relationships in nature.
_____ I feel closer to God when I am surrounded by nature.
_____ I notice similarities and differences in flowers, birds, trees, and other things in nature.
_____ I like to pray using natural objects (example: a flower, rock, or leaf).
_____ I see God in all created things.
_____ ***Total for Section 6***

Section 7

_____ I prefer to pray alone.
_____ I regularly spend time reflecting or meditating about important questions in my life.
_____ I have specific goals in life that I am working toward.
_____ I have the courage of my convictions and am not easily influenced by others.
_____ I have great inner strength.

_____ I recognize that I am responsible for all that I say and do.
_____ I enjoy learning about myself.
_____ I am a very private person.
_____ I am honest about my own strengths and weaknesses.
_____ I prefer silence when I pray.
_____ *Total for Section 7*

Section 8

_____ I enjoy participating in prayer groups.
_____ Being with other people energizes me.
_____ I enjoy learning about how people pray across different cultures.
_____ People often come to me for advice.
_____ I am a natural leader.
_____ I usually talk over my questions and concerns with a friend.
_____ I enjoy participating in Bible study groups.
_____ I like to bring groups of people together for shared prayer and reflection.
_____ I am or would like to be part of a prayer group which meets regularly.
_____ I enjoy sharing my reflections and insights with others.
_____ *Total for Section 8*

Part II

Add your scores in each category, and multiply each score by 10. Then plot the results on the bar graph below.

100									
90									
80									
70									
60									
50									
40									
30									
20									
10									
		Section 1	Section 2	Section 3	Section 4	Section 5	Section 6	Section 7	Section 8

Part III

Key:

Section 1 reflects the Verbal-Linguistic prayer style.

Section 2 reflects the Logical-Mathematic prayer style.

Section 3 reflects the Visual-Spatial prayer style.

Section 4 reflects the Musical-Rhythmic prayer style.

Section 5 reflects the Bodily-Kinesthetic prayer style.

Section 6 reflects the Naturalist prayer style.

Section 7 reflects the Intrapersonal prayer style.

Section 8 reflects the Interpersonal prayer style.

*My preferred prayer style(s) is(are)*________________.

Finding God through words
CHAPTER ONE

"The words that enlighten the soul are more precious than jewels."

—Hazrat Inayat Khan

Finding God through words

Words have long been a part of our prayer and worship traditions. The Divine Office, the missal, Sacred Scripture, and spiritual reading books have provided powerful ways of interacting with the Divine. They have enabled the articulation of mystery, hope, joy, sorrow, comfort, and a myriad of other emotions and feelings about God. For some, words strengthen religious convictions and provid a tool for growth in their spiritual lives. These are the verbal-linguistic learners.

For these learners, words inspire and motivate, stimulate and encourage. They provide a pathway to explore the deepest realities of life. The Divine is sensed through the words on a page that can express the thoughts and beliefs at the core of one's existence.

Reading invites one to enter a sacred space to share in the wisdom of others. The phrase "breaking open the word" is especially meaningful to one who is verbally-linguistically gifted because words have such power to transform. Whether reading Scripture, poetry, or a spiritual reading book, this learner's prayer life is enriched.

Writing provides another avenue for self-discovery and the discovery of the God within. Words put to paper help to clarify and make concrete abstract ideas and concepts. They facilitate personal expression and provide a vehicle for self-understanding. Writing becomes prayer as the pen and paper reveal the interconnectedness of God and his creation.

Speaking and listening also nurture and give life to the verbally-linguistically gifted. They are alternate mediums that use words to convey and take in information. Speaking aloud about one's beliefs or listening to another share his or hers opens up new pathways to prayer and is a means of growth and transformation, both personally and communally.

A spiritual autobiography

"Days are like scrolls: write on them only what you want remembered."

—Bachya ibn Pakuda

A spiritual autobiography is the story of your relationship to God—the path from birth to where you are now. The following questions invite you to reflect and write about your personal spiritual journey.

Do you remember the first time you thought about God?

What are your earliest memories of God?

Who are some people who have nurtured your faith throughout your life? How did they do so?

Where are the places in your life that are sacred for you? Is there a special place now?

Recall times throughout your life when God felt very close. How did you feel at those times?

Recall times throughout your life when God felt far away. How did you feel during those times?

How has your faith been tested?

How has your faith changed?

How has your faith grown?

How important is spirituality in your life right now?

What are you doing to nurture your faith today?

How do you spend time with God each day?

What style of prayer is life-giving and nurturing for you?

As you look at yourself in the present moment, what are some of your hopes and dreams? Perhaps it would be helpful to think of the different areas of your life and the goals you have in each—family, work, education/intellectual, social, spiritual, and financial.

How have you fit God into your goals?

Storytelling

"Storytelling is so natural to human beings it suggests a definition:
we are the creatures who think in stories."
—John & Mary Harrell

Storytelling is part of the tradition of peoples throughout the world extending back to our earliest ancestors. Gathered around fires in the mountains and forests, by lakes and rivers, in the deserts and the swamplands, people would gather to listen to the stories of the elders. The wisdom of the people passed from generation to generation through this oral tradition.

The origin of the universe, the people, all living beings, the rocks and hills, oceans and sky became the subject of the stories. The earliest human awareness of a divine presence lived in the stories, and the knowledge of his love for the earth and all creation and his desire for us to live in harmony were passed down to this day.

Each generation has its own stories. Most people no longer gather around campfires to hear stories, but we read stories that have been written down to help us remember. Stories can entertain, delight, challenge, encourage, and enlighten. They can touch deep and hidden recesses within our own beings. They provide a lens through which we view the world and call forth a response to the events of our own day. Stories frequently cross cultures or invite comparisons to stories in other cultures.

Prayer: Read or listen to a story, and respond orally or in writing.

Questions for Discussion or Reflective Writing
(for use with any story):

1. *What truth does this story reveal to me?*

2. *How can I apply this story to my own life?*

3. *How did this story celebrate the best in human nature?*

4. *Where did I find God in this story?*

5. *How am I challenged by this story?*

Add your own questions:

Children's stories for all ages

De Paola , Tomie. *The Clown of God: An Old Story*. Harcourt, 1989.

___________ *The Legend of the Indian Paintbrush*. Scott Foresman, 1996.

___________ *The Legend of the Bluebonnet*. Paper Star Publishers, 1996.

___________ *The Legend of the Poinsettia*. Paper Star Publishers, 1997.

Frasier, Debra. *On the Day You Were Born*. Harcourt, 1991.

Paulus, Trina. *Hope for the Flowers*. Paulist Press, 1973.

Rylant, Cynthia. *The Dreamer.* The Blue Sky Press: An Imprint of Scholastic, Inc., 1993.

Schimmel, Schim. *Dear Children of the Earth*. NorthWord Press, Inc., 1994.

Silverstein, Shel. *The Missing Piece*. HarperCollins, 1976.

___________ *The Giving Tree*. HarperCollins, 1964

Swartz, Nancy Sohn. *In Our Image: God's First Creatures*. Jewish Lights Publications, 1998.

Wood, Douglas. *Old Turtle*. Scholastic, 2001.

Story collections

Bausch, William J., *A World of Stories for Preachers and Teachers: And All Who Love Stories That Move and Challenge*. Twenty-Third Publications, 1998.

Cavanaugh, Brian T.O.R., *The Sower's Seeds*. Paulist Press, 1990.

Gray, Alice (editor). *Stories for the Heart*. Multnomah Books, 2002.

Larned, Marianne (editor). *Stone Soup for the World: Life-Changing Stories of Ordinary Kindness and Courageous Acts of Service*. Conari Press, 1998.

Litherland, Janet. *Storytelling from the Bible: Making Scripture Live for All Ages through the Art of Storytelling*. Meriwether Publishers, 1991.

Shea, John. *The Legend of the Bells and Other Tales* ACTA Publications, 1997.

Shaw, Susan M., *Storytelling in Religious Education*. Religious Education Press, 1999.

Song, Choan-Seng. *The Believing Heart: An Invitation to Story Theology*. Fortress Press, 1999.

White, William. *Stories for Telling: A Treasury for Christian Storytellers*. Augsburg Fortress Press, 1990.

Parables

Jesus knew the power of story. He was a magnificent storyteller. He clothed the most profound thoughts in the everyday language of the people. The parables talked of pearls and seeds, fig trees and coins, and vineyards and wedding feasts, yet beneath the ordinary words lay the deepest of truths. Jesus' parables were powerful precisely because they were simple. They still serve as a compelling tool for prayer today.

Prayer: Read one of the parables, and allow the words to wash over you. Enter into the story. Become a participant. Go to the wedding or be a laborer in the vineyard. Lose a coin or search for your lost sheep.

Parables

- Introduction to the Parables (Matthew 13:1–3, 10–17)
- The Sower (Matthew 13:3–9; Mark 4:3–9; Luke 8:5–8)
- The Lamp (Mark 4:21–23; Luke 8:16–18)
- The Good Samaritan (Luke 10:30–37)
- The Barren Fig Tree (Luke 13:6–9)
- The Measure (Mark 4:24–25)
- The Darnel (Matthew 13:24–30)
- The Mustard Seed (Matthew 13:31–32; Mark 4:30–32; Luke 13:18–19)
- The Yeast (Matthew 13:33; Luke 13:20–21)
- The Treasure and the Pearl (Matthew 13:44–46)
- The Dragnet (Matthew 13:47–50)
- The Lost Sheep (Matthew 18:12–14; Luke 15:4–7)
- The Lost Coin (Luke 15:8–10)
- The Prodigal Son (Luke 15:11–32)
- The Unforgiving Debtor (Matthew 18:23–35)
- The Rich Young Man (Matthew 19:16–22; Mark 10:17–22)
- The Vineyard Laborers (Matthew 20:1–16)
- The Two Sons (Matthew 21:28–31)
- The Wicked Husbandmen (Matthew 21:33–41; Luke 20:9–16)
- The Wedding Feast (Matthew 22:1–14)
- The Conscientious Steward (Matthew 24:45–51)
- The Ten Bridesmaids (Matthew 25:1–13)
- The Talents (Matthew 25:14–30)
- The Crafty Steward (Luke 16:1–8)
- The Pounds (Luke 19:11–27)

The parables touched the people of Jesus' day because the ordinary people could identify with the words and images. Fig trees and drachmas do not convey concrete images today because they do not reflect our experience. However, the central truths of the parables, the messages about the Kingdom of God, have not changed. These messages are as important for us as they were for the people of Bethlehem, Judea, and Galilee.

Prayer: After reflecting on one of the parables, revise it to use language and images that are common to people of the 21st century.

A few points to remember:

1. *Note the setting of the parable.*
2. *Note the characters in the parable.*
3. *Determine the main points of the parable.*
4. *Think about how the parable conveys an important part of Jesus' teaching.*
5. *Apply the main ideas to a similar situation in today's society.*

-A retelling of the Parable of the Good Samaritan

The young man checked the address on his pad to make sure he was delivering the pizza to the right house. As he stood under the streetlight near his car, several gang members jumped him from behind, beat him up, and ran off with the pizza and his wallet.

A while later, a businessman hurrying home from work saw the man lying in the gutter, but didn't take the time to stop because he was late for dinner.

An hour or so later a local pastor crossed the street near where the man lay, but he didn't stop because he was on his way to an ecumenical prayer service at a local church.

An illegal immigrant working at a local factory saw the man as she walked home from work and had pity on him. Although she was afraid of the INS, she called the police and waited with the man until they arrived.

Which of these three showed compassion and treated the man as a neighbor?

Use space below:

Finding the sacred in poetry

"Poetry is a kind of medication that slows me down and brings me back to myself."

—Allen Ginsberg

Poetry touches the soul. It is the language of the heart which inspires us to see the world anew. It leads us to depths that rational thinking cannot. It weaves the threads of human emotions into a magnificent tapestry of words. Poetry gives voice to images of the Infinite through a dazzling interplay between nouns and verbs, adjectives and adverbs, prepositions and conjunctions. The words call and beckon us to follow into the well of meaning wherein lies the waters that refresh and herald new life.

Prayer: Choose one of the following poems (or excerpt from a poem), or find one of your own to use for meditation. Say the words slowly to yourself or aloud, allowing them to enter your heart. What images of God do the words evoke?

i thank you God for most this amazing day:
for the leaping greenly spirits of trees and a
blue true dream of sky; and for everything
which is natural which is infinite which is
yes...

—E. E. Cummings

I Fly!

You big, bright beautiful God,
this is my day for flying!
I reach out to the bigness of you.
I touch the brightness of you
and I feel the beauty of you
in the center of my living.
Today your bear me up, up,
past my doubts about both of us,
to the certainty of your love.

Today, God, I know you.
All those words I learned are burnt in your fire.
You are sun to my Icarus,
candle to my moth.
Today I fly
and am dissolved in you...!

And if tomorrow I am grounded
by a weight of anxieties,
if my feet are heavy and there are clouds
between me and the sun,
then let me keep hold
of the warm place in my heart
reminding me that today I flew
and was kissed by God.

—Joy Cowley
(New Zealand)

Apprehend God in all things, for God is in all things.

Every single creature is full of God and is a book about God.

Every creature is a word of God.

If I spent enough time with the tiniest creature — even a caterpillar — I would never have to prepare a sermon. So full of God is every creature.

—Meister Eckart (Germany)

Take time to listen to the birds,
the waves,
the wind.

Take time to breathe in the air,
the earth,
the ocean.

Take time to be still,
to be silent
to allow God to fill you up
with deep peace and love.

—Mairead Maguire (Ireland)
Nobel Peace Prize Laureate

Grandfather,
Look at our brokenness.

We know that in all Creation,
Only the human family
Has strayed from the Sacred Way.

We know that we are the ones
Who are divided
And we are the ones
Who must come back together
To walk in the Sacred Way.

Grandfather,
Sacred One,
Teach us love, compassion, honor
That we may heal the earth
And heal each other.

—Native American
(Ojibway)

Prayer: Make a collection of poems which speak to you of the sacred. Explore poems from a variety of cultures to more fully comprehend the universality of the quest for God. Pray for the people whose poems you have chosen, and allow yourself to walk with them in the Sacred Way.

Creative prayer through poetic forms

"Through metaphor we pass from one state of knowing into the next,
ever experimenting, ever creating, ever flowing, as the universe does."
—Burghild Nina Holzer

Spiritual Metaphors

Metaphors are threads which connect our inner and outer knowing. They are not confined by our cognitive knowledge but allow us to walk among the stars and give words to our heart's thoughts. The abstract becomes more knowable through metaphoric speech by building a bridge of words between the natural and the spiritual.

Prayer: Choose a metaphor to describe Jesus.

Jesus is the flute whose melody my heart follows.

Jesus is the eagle on whose back I soar.

My own metaphors:

Variation: Try metaphors on other spiritual topics, such as God, Mary, and the saints.

Lanterne

The lanterne is a five-line poem designed in the shape of a Japanese lantern. It can be done with a set number of syllables per line (1, 2, 3, 4, 1) or a set number of words per line (1, 2, 3, 4, 1).

Spirit,
Invite me
To join you
In recreating the world.
Transformation.

I
freely desire
to give all
to build your Kingdom,
Lord.

Prayer: Create your own lanterne by using the space provided on the right.

My own lanterne:

Haiku

Japanese haiku consists of three lines with a syllabic pattern of 5-7-5. Haiku are always about nature.

Not a leaf stirring
Listen to the nothingness
Hear the voice of God.

I see myself now
Poised, still, ready to begin
The inward journey.

Casuarina pines
Gently bowing to the earth
Give praise to their God.

Light green, dark green leaves
Pine-coned, fruited, flowering trees
All signs of God's love.

Prayer: Write your haiku, giving praise to God for a wonder in creation.

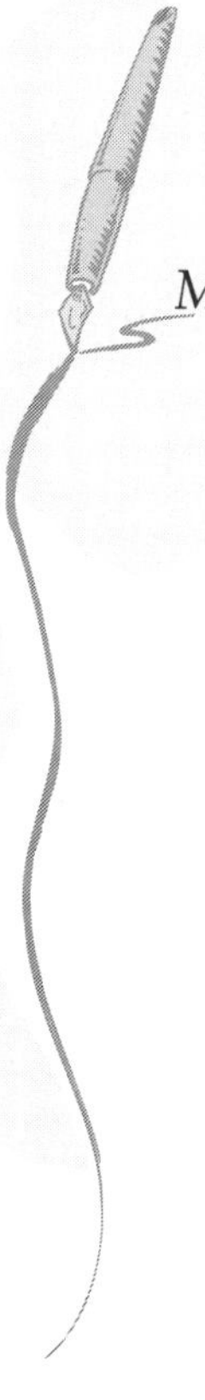

My own haiku:

Tanka

Tanka is an extension of haiku. It is about nature and has a syllabic pattern of 5-7-5-7-7. Begin with a haiku, and extend it!

Renga

Renga is a Japanese poem written by several persons. The first part, a haiku (5-7-5), is written by one person, and another person writes the next two lines (7-7). Another person writes the next part (5-7-5), and yet another writes the next two lines (7-7). This pattern repeats throughout the renga.

Cinquain

Standard pattern:

One word, a title
Two words to describe the title
Three words to tell an action
Four words to tell a feeling
One word to refer to the title.

Spirit
Empowering, Inspiring
Sends me forth
Strengthened for the task
Guide

Prayer: Create your own *cinquain* by following the pattern.

My own haiku:

—A Five Senses Poem

Love

Love is yellow like the sun.
It sounds like gentle rain on a summer's eve.
It tastes like marshmallows from the campfire
And smells like roses in the midst of winter.
Love looks like the stars in a Caribbean sky.
It makes me feel alive.

Prayer: Write a five-senses poem in the space below. Choose an emotion, a quality, a person, or an idea that is important to you. Then follow the formula below.

Line 1: Tell about the subject's color.

Line 2: Tell what it sounds like.

Line 3: Tell what it tastes like.

Line 4: Tell what it smells like.

Line 5: Tell what it looks like.

Line 6: Tell how it makes you feel.

Use space below:

Figurative Comparisons

A figurative comparison is simple two-line poem in which you express your widom.

I used to worry that my work was not perfect.
But now I rejoice in the creativity that allows for messiness.

Prayer: Express a piece of wisdom that life has taught you.

I used to:

But now I:

Use space below:

Proverbs to prayer

Proverbs are the windows to a culture's soul. They are born out of the experiences of a people and hold the wisdom which nurtures and sustains life. They provide insight into the minds and hearts of a people and convey the values and assumptions upon which life is lived and decisions are made. Proverbs can also lead us to prayer by inviting us to let go of our logical, rational explanations for reality and inviting us to enter into heart space.

Prayer: Choose one or more of the following proverbs, and let it enter your heart space. What is the kernel of truth which resonates with you? Pray silently for the grace to accept the wisdom of the proverb.

This can be done as an individual prayer, but the proverbs can also be springboards for discussion and journal entries.

Listen, or thy tongue will keep thee deaf.

—Native American

Envious people never compliment; they only swallow.

—Mexico

Everyone is the age of his or her heart.

—Guatemala

You make the road by walking it.

—Nicaragua

The devil tempts but doesn't force.

—Guyana

Little by little, one walks far.

—Peru

Hands that give also receive.

—Ecuador

Abundance and scarcity are never far apart; the rich and the poor frequent the same house.

—Somalia

Blessed are those who can please themselves.

—South Africa
(Zulu)

Earth is but a marketplace; heaven is home.

—West Africa
(Yoruba)

The giver should forget, but the receiver should remember forever.

—Poland

Life is like the moon: now dark, now full.

—Poland

Wisdom is easy to carry but difficult to gather.

—Czechoslovakia

The God who gave us teeth will also give us bread.

—Czechoslovakia

Give good, and get good.

—Estonia

Call on God, but row away from the rocks.

—India

If you take the field of an enemy, the enemy will come and take your field.

—Mesopotamia

Patience is power; with time and patience the mulberry leaf becomes silk.

—China

A turtle travels only when it sticks its neck out.

—Korea

Cultivate a heart of love that knows no anger.

—Cambodia

When eating a fruit, think of the person who planted the tree.

—Vietnam

Unless you call out, who will open the door?

—Ethiopia.

The proverb I chose:

My thoughts:

Spiritual journaling

"A journal is a tool for self-discovery, an aid to concentration, a mirror for the soul, a place to generate and capture ideas, a safety valve for the emotions, a training ground for the writer, and a good friend and confidant."

—Ronald Klug
How to Keep a Spiritual Journal

Keeping a journal is neither a novel nor a new idea. Journals have been kept in a variety of forms since the beginning of time. Our ancestors left accounts of their lives on the walls of caves; explorers left ships' logs detailing their voyages; the evangelists wrote about events during Jesus' time on earth; and Paul left numerous letters about his journeys and the life of the early church.

Journaling gives us a tool to articulate our innermost thoughts and feelings. It provides us with a vehicle to capture the events of our daily lives and to search for the deeper meanings underlying our actions and our interactions with others. Journaling can lead us to prayer by providing a safe space for our inner voice—the voice we use to talk with God.

Prayer: Try one or more of the journaling activities listed below.

Stream of Consciousness

Take a few minutes each day to jot down in your journal the ideas that are on your mind or anything that is bothering you. Let the ideas spread across the paper in no particular order. Don't worry about grammar or spelling. Simply allow your thoughts, feelings, and emotions to tumble out.

Newspaper Prayer

Choose a headline from a newspaper, and paste it in your journal. Use it as a starting point for prayer. Enter into the lives of the people for whom you are praying, and allow yourself to feel their joys and pains. Become one with your brothers and sisters throughout the world.

Quotes: Select a famous quotation that is meaningful to you, and reflect upon it. Write your thoughts in your journal. Choose one of the following, or find one of your own.

"The heart of difference between the modern world and the traditional one is that in traditional societies people are a valuable resource and the interrelations between them are carefully tended; in modern society things are valuable and people are all too often treated as disposable."

—David Maybury-Lewis

"Do what you can, with what you have, where you are."

—Theodore Roosevelt

"When you decide to give yourself to a great cause, you must arrive at the point where no sacrifice is too great."

—Coretta Scott King

"You can't change the world. You can only change yourself."

—Beatrice Wood

"I believe we are here on planet Earth to live, grow up, and do what we can to make this world a better place for all people to enjoy freedom."

—Rosa Parks

"To be nobody but yourself—in a world which is doing its best, night and day, to make you everybody else—means to fight the hardest battle any human being can fight; and never stop fighting."

—E.E. Cummings

"In the rush and noise of life…step within yourself and be still. Wait upon God and feel his good presence; this will carry you through your day's business."

—William Penn

"It was our belief that love of possessions is a weakness to be overcome. Its appeal is to the material part, and if allowed its way, it will in time disturb one's spiritual balance."

—Ohiyesa
(Charles Eastman)
Sioux Writer and Elder

"I think we would be able to live in this world more peaceably if our spirituality were to come from looking not just into infinity but very closely at the world around us—and appreciating its depth and divinity."

—Thomas Moore

"We are children of Mother Earth and we were sent different areas to take care of, to use our language, our ceremonies, whatever we develop to help keep this land life in balance."

—Thomas Banyacya
(Hopi Elder)

"Peace is not a concept, it is the way the Creator expects us to live. When I am not living peacefully among others, I must look to myself to see why I am out of harmony, because harmony is the natural order."

—Anne Wilson Schaef

"To keep a lamp burning we have to keep putting oil in it."

—Mother Theresa

"In times of major change and social stress, people are challenged to stand up for what they believe. Perhaps this is the hidden blessing released by the suffering of the world."

—Elizabeth Roberts
& Elias Amidon

The past may become either an opportunity or an obstacle. Everything depends on what we make of it and not what it makes of us.

—Sarvepalli Radhakrishnan

Gratitude Journals

Keep a journal by your bed. Each evening write in it those things for which you are truly grateful that occurred in your life that day. Ending the day with listing the things for which you are grateful will help lead to a restful night's sleep. Rereading your gratitude journal periodically helps you see the good that is happening in your life and automatically leads you to praise God, who has made it all possible.

Letters to God

Take some time each day to write a letter to God. What are the things in your heart that you most need to share with someone you can trust? Write as you would to a dear friend whom you know understands you and loves you no matter what you do or say.

Interview God

Write a list of questions that you would like to have answered. Ask God about them, and write the answers you think God might have for your questions.

What do you think, God, about poverty?

What do you think about the environment?

How can I respond in love to someone who hates me?

What do you really want me to do with my life?

My own questions:

You Are There

Read a passage from the New Testament and put yourself in the scene. Write as though you are with Paul on one of his journeys or with Mary standing at the foot of the cross. Let your words reflect your thoughts and feelings as you find yourself walking the Earth more than 2,000 years ago.

A potpourri of creative writing ideas for prayer

A–Z Prayer

Take a few moments to think about the many ways God speaks to you through the people and daily events of your life. Make an A–Z list of words or phrases, such as the one begun below, that remind you of God's presence in your life.

A—Anhinga (tropical bird)
B—Beaches
C—Clouds
D—Daylily

Prayer: Choose one of the entries from your list, and think about it. What meaning does it have for you? How does it speak of God to you? Give thanks for it.

Interview

Choose a character from the Bible, and interview him or her. Talk to the character about the situations in your world. Look at how this character responded to the events of his or her time, and write a dialogue between the two of you about responding to a crisis in the world today.

Prayer: After you have finished writing the interview, ask God to give you the courage and strength to respond to a crisis in your world with the same courage and conviction with which your Bible character responded.

How-To Manual

Write a how-to manual for someone who would like to be a Christian. What are the materials needed? What are the directions to follow?

Prayer: Are you following the directions in God's manual? Talk with God about your desire to be faithful, and ask for the grace to follow the blueprint God has for your life.

Prayer Flash Cards

Create a set of flash cards with positive actions.

Prayer: Choose one card each day, and do the action described.

Thank God for flowers today.

Thank God for a special friend today.

Say a prayer today for someone you don't care for.

Call someone today who is lonely.

Word Splash

Choose a person such as God, the Holy Spirit, Jesus, or a favorite saint or Bible character. Write it in the center of a sheet of paper, and draw a circle around it. Brainstorm as many qualities and ideas as you can think of that describe that person. Splash the words all over the page in different handwriting styles and in different directions.

Prayer: Choose any one of the descriptive words, and reflect on how that quality or idea is/was present in the life of the person. Ask God to give you that gift in your own life.

Chapter one resources

Cowley, Joy. *Aotearoa Psalms: Prayers of a New People*. Catholic Supplies New Zealand, Ltd., 1989.

Fadiman, Clifton (editor). *The Little, Brown Book of Anecdotes*. Little, Brown and Company, 1985.

Fox, John. *Finding What You Didn't Lose: Expressing Your Truth and Creativity Through Poem-Making*. J. P. Tarcher/Putnam, 1995.

Jones, Shirley Ann (editor) *Simply Living: The Spirit of the Indigenous People*. New World Library, 1999.

Klug, Ronald. *How to Keep a Spiritual Journal*. Augsburg Fortress Press, 1993.

Kovacs, Edna. *Writing Across Cultures: A Handbook on Writing Poetry and Lyrical Prose*. Blue Heron Publishing, Inc., 1994.

Lorie, Peter and Manuela Dunn Mascetti (editors). *The Quotable Spirit*. Castle Books, 2000.

Malecka, Janina. *The Multicultural Treasury*. J. Weston Walch, Publisher, 1993.

Roberts, Elizabeth and Elias Amidon (editors). *Earth Prayers from Around the World*. Harper SanFrancisco, 1991.

___________________. *Prayers for a Thousand Years*. Harper San Francisco, 1999.

___________________. *Life Prayers from Around the World*. Harper San Francisco, 1996.

Schaef, Anne Wilson. *Native Wisdom for White Minds*. Ballantine Books, 1995.

Sweeney, Jacqueline. *Incredible Quotations*. Scholastic, Inc., 1997.

Tirabassi, Maren C. and Kathy Wonson Eddy. *Gifts of Many Cultures: Worship Resources for the Global Community*. Pilgrim Press, 1995.

Wood, Nancy (editor). *The Serpent's Tongue: Prose, Poetry, and Art of the New Mexico Pueblos*. Dutton, 1997.

Finding God through math & logic

CHAPTER TWO

"Mathematics is the handwriting on the human consciousness of the very Spirit of Life itself."

—Claude Bragdon

Finding God through math & logic

Mathematics is more than just the computation of numbers. The logical-mathematic mind perceives objects and their functions in the environment, uses abstract symbols to represent concrete objects and concepts, and solves problems through logic. This learner also sees patterns and relationships among diverse phenomena and seeks to find answers by gathering evidence, making and testing hypotheses, and formulating models.

The logical-mathematic intelligence is highly valued in western culture, which can seem to presume that all problems can be solved through analyzing the component parts. This is one way to solve problems; but as the other intelligences demonstrate, there are many ways of solving problems. Not all solutions are the results of rational analysis. However, there are many elements of the logical-mathematic mind that can lead to a deep prayer life.

Prayer that is most satisfying for the logical-mathematical individual often follows patterns. Many of our traditional forms of worship, such as the rosary, Mass, and the Stations of the Cross, follow logical and well-established sequential order, which gives the individual a sense of comfort and peace. However, this gifted mind can also deal with abstractions and imagination. Exploring this intelligence more deeply through a variety of alternative prayer options can lead to higher levels of understanding that ultimately can lead to a deeper relationship with God.

The logical-mathematic form of prayer invites us to see the connections that are present every day as a way to help us know God. It beckons us to follow a logical path to reach a point that is beyond our reasoning.

A simple counting prayer

"Where there is number, there is beauty."
—Proclus

God is full of surprises. Everyday in a thousand different ways, God can be found in the most unexpected yet ordinary places. Oftentimes, we are so busy looking for God that we fail to see the Divine Presence in all that surrounds us.

This prayer invites us to look at the ordinary and see the extraordinary right before our eyes. It is a prayer of consciousness, of awareness. God enjoins us to "Be still and know that I am God." From the first glimmering light of dawn until blackness invades the night landscape, God is trying to get our attention to say "I love you."

A Simple Counting Prayer

1. *an empty boat by the lake's shore inviting me to risk letting go*

2. *a brilliant red cardinal warbling in the branches of the oak tree*

3. *a child laughing*

4. *the different shades of green on the leaves of the trees in my yard*

5. *the pen I am holding that reminds me that God wants to write on my heart*

6. *the computer in front of me that connects me to the world and reminds me that in God all is connected*

7. *the words to a song on the radio*

8. *a rock lying next to the sidewalk*

9. *a cloud in the sky*

10. *a raindrop*

Prayer: When you get up in the morning, count slowly from one to ten to remind yourself that today you are going to see the presence of God in at least ten different things. Make a simple list numbered from 1 to 10. Throughout the day, stop for moments of awareness and jot down words or phrases about your observations. In the evening take a few minutes to review your list, and ask yourself "How was God present to me today?" Reflect on only one item, on several items, or the whole list. Thank God for the gift of his presence in the ordinary.

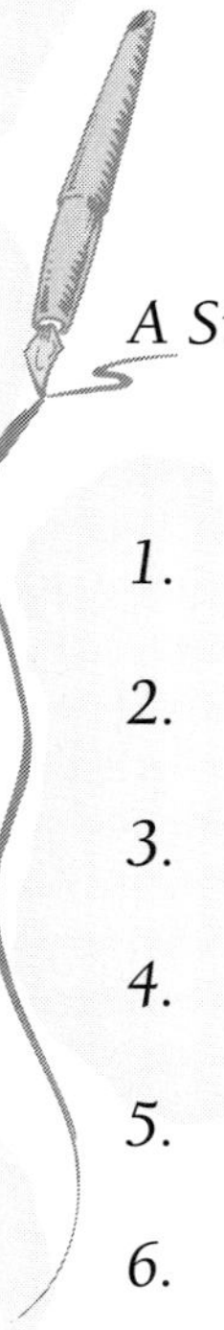

A Simple Counting Prayer:

1.

2.

3.

4.

5.

6.

7.

8.

9.

10.

Scripture and peace

"What we know is not much. What we do not know is immense."
—Pierre-Simon de Laplaces

Mathematicians and scientists are concerned with gathering evidence, making hypotheses, formulating models, and building strong arguments. To approach prayer with a mathematical mind is to seek truth by looking at the facts. Prayer invites us to model our lives on Jesus. What was his life like? Where do we go to find the information about how we should live our lives? The Bible is our source book and provides very reliable data to guide our decision-making.

Prayer: Choose one or more of the following Scripture passages for prayer, and allow them to speak to your heart about how God is calling you to live a life of peace.

Peace

- Matthew 5:9
- Matthew 7:12
- Matthew 11:28–30
- Matthew 18:21–22
- Mark 11:20–25
- Mark 12:28cc
- John 8:32
- John 14:27
- John 16:33
- Acts 10:36
- Romans 12:19
- Romans 15:13
- Ephesians 2:17
- Ephesians 4:4
- Colossians 1:20
- Colossians 3:12–15
- I Thessalonians 5:23
- II Thessalonians 3:16

A few questions to reflect on:

What does the passage say to me about God?

Am I at peace with myself?

Am I at peace with my family?

Who are the people with whom I am not at peace?

How can I be a peacemaker in my world today?

The calendar prayer

Each day God invites us to live lives of love and service. The invitation is always there, but with our busy schedules we often fail to remember to acknowledge God's call through our daily actions. The weekly calendar prayer is designed to help us take a proactive stance by writing down one deliberate action to do each day to live out our Christian commitment.

Some examples:

Do a random act of kindness.

Say the rosary.

Take a few minutes to appreciate some thing beautiful in nature.

Say "I love you" to a family member.

Listen to a song that praises God.

Do ten minutes of spiritual reading.

Prayer: Design a weekly calendar such as the one below. Use the calendar to plan a specific action for each day to deepen your relationship with God. Put it in a prominent place, and check it each morning to remind yourself of the day's commitment.

the week of ____________

Sunday	
Monday	
Tuesday	
Wednesday	
Thursday	
Friday	
Saturday	

The prayer of ups and downs

"Life's inevitable changes are like a compulsory roller-coaster ride. You can cower and shut your eyes tight, or you can exult in the thrills."

—Roger Crawford

Life is filled with ups and downs, joys and sorrows. There are bumps and curves, hills and valleys. No one is immune to the constantly changing panorama of life. Oftentimes, the bumps catch us unaware and toss us about like seeds in the wind. We seem to have no control and simply allow ourselves to be carried along with the current.

The ups and downs, however, are indeed filled with meaning if only we have the eyes and take the time to see what it is they have to teach. There is a pattern to our lives that will reveal itself to us and show us the presence of God in the very ordinary days of our lives.

Prayer One: Choose a character in the Bible. The character can be male or female and from the Old or the New Testament. Read the passages that mention him or her, and jot down major events in the person's life.

When you have finished reading and recording the person's life events, number a sheet of graph paper 1–10 along the vertical axis. Then choose eight to ten events from your notes, and give each of them a value from 1 to 10 (with 1 as the lowest point and 10 as the highest). Plot the numbers on the graph, and label each point with a letter. Along the horizontal axis, write an identifying word to correspond to each point.

Then connect the dots, and look at the highs and lows in the person's life. Reflect on the significance of the events at the highest points as well as those at the lowest points. How did this person allow God to transform his or her life? How was God present in the highs and the lows of this person's life?

Thank God for the gifts this individual gave to the world and for allowing this person to touch your life by revealing one pattern of the divine in action.

Prayer Two: Look at your own life over the course of the past day, week, month, or year or more. Write down the highs and lows during the period you have chosen. Assign a 1-to-10 value to the events, and graph them as you did for the Bible character.

How has God touched you in the events of your life? What was different about the high points and the low points? What do you learn about yourself as you look back over the period of time that you graphed? How was God present during the difficult times? How did you acknowledge God's presence during the down times? How was God present during times of joy? How did you acknowledge God's presence during the up times? Is there a pattern to your life? What does the pattern look like?

Thank God for being present in all the events of your life, even during those times when you least felt the divine presence.

Problem-solving prayer

"Chance favors only the prepared mind."
—Louis Pasteur

Word problems are often the most difficult math problems to solve because they require not only knowledge of the mechanics of math, but also the capacity to organize the information and formulate a problem. The following are sample questions one might ask when organizing information to solve a math word problem:

What do I know?

What don't I know?

What do I need to know?

How can I find out?

What is the real problem?

What are the parts of the problem?

What are the characteristics of the problem?

Have I seen others like it?

What strategy worked then?

What strategy do I need now?

This logical, orderly process of thinking can also be applied to problems we encounter in life. Breaking a problem down by asking questions like those above can give new insights and provide answers for dilemmas in life.

Prayer: Choose something occurring in your life right now which is problematic or about which you seek clarity. Find a quiet place to reflect on your personal concern.

What do I know about the problem or concern?

What are aspects of the problem or concern that I don't know about?

What further information do I need?

How can I find the information I need?

What do I see as the crux of the problem?

Can I break down the problem into parts?

What are the characteristics of this problem or concern?

Have I encountered other situations like this in my life?

What strategy worked for me before?

Will that same strategy work in this situation, or do I need a new strategy?

Thank God for the new insights you gain during this prayer, and resolve to use those insights to take positive action.

Math and logic: quotes to ponder

Prayer: Find a comfortable place to reflect on one or more of the following quotations. Allow God to speak to you and lead you to new insights through thoughts about math and logic.

"The mathematical sciences particularly exhibit order, symmetry, and limitation; and these are the greatest forms of the beautiful."

—Aristotle

"Life is a school of probability."

—Walter Bagehot

"God is like a skillful Geometrician."

—Sir Thomas Browne

"You can only find truth with logic if you have already found truth without it."

—G. K. Chesterton

"The composer opens the cage door for arithmetic; the draftsman gives geometry its freedom."

—Cocteau

"We used to think that if we knew one, we knew two, because one and one are two. We are finding that we must learn a great deal more about 'and.'"

—Sir Arthur Eddington

"God does not care about our mathematical difficulties. He integrates empirically."

—Albert Einstein

"From the intrinsic evidence of his creation, the Great Architect of the Universe now begins to appear as a pure mathematician."

—Sir James Jeans

"The chief aim of all investigations of the external world should be to discover the rational order and harmony which has been imposed on it by God and which He revealed to us in the language of mathematics."

—Johannes Kepler

"The imaginary number is a fine and wonderful recourse of the divine spirit, almost an amphibian between being and not being."

—Gottfried Leibniz

Names of God

"I have called you by name, you are mine."
—Isaiah 43:1

In Hebrew tradition the name of a person is sacred. A name was believed to hold the spirit of a person, and knowing someone's name indicated a special knowledge of that person. We know that in the Old Testament, the name of God was never spoken aloud. Yet the concept of the name was so important that it was mentioned 800 times in the Old Testament and 180 times in the New Testament.

Throughout Scripture, God is referred to by many names. Reflecting on the different names of God can help us see the depth of God's relationship with us. At various points in our lives, certain names may have more significance to us, but praying with the names by which God is called can give new insights into how the Divine chooses to enter our lives.

Prayer: Choose one of the names of Jesus below, and spend quiet time in prayer. Allow yourself to see how Jesus invites you into a deeper understanding of himself through these names. What does the name tell you about Jesus' relationship with you? With others? How does this name call you to be in relationship to Jesus? To others?

Bread	*John 6: 35, 51*
Comforter	*Luke 4: 38–39*
Light	*John 8: 12*
Master	*Luke 5: 1–11*
Door	*John 10: 7, 9*
Healer	*Luke 5: 12–14*

Shepherd of sinners	*John 10: 11, 14* *Matthew 9: 10–13*
Friend	*Luke 5: 29–32*
Life	*John 11: 25*
Challenger	*Luke 6: 24–26*
Truth	*John 14: 6*
Integrity	*Matthew 21: 28–32*
Way	*John 14: 6*
Justice	*Matthew 25: 31–46*
Vine	*John 15: 1,5*
Friend of poor & children	*Luke 14: 12–14* *Luke 18: 15–17* *John 4: 1–30*
Beloved	*Luke 3:22*
Servant	*John 13: 1–20*
Prophet	*Luke 4: 16–24* *Luke 12: 1–12*
Teacher	*Luke 4: 31–32* *Luke 19: 47–48*

Prayer using Bloom's taxonomy

"Imagination is more important than knowledge."
—Albert Einstein

Bloom's taxonomy[1] has long been used in education to develop critical thinking. Benjamin Bloom divided cognitive development into six main levels: knowledge, comprehension, application, analysis, synthesis, and evaluation. Each succeeding level requires a deeper level of thought. The lower-level questions are more simple and factual, while the higher-level ones are more complex and conceptual. According to Vowery Dodd Carlile, "The highest levels are seldom used; they are more difficult to write and, because they have no definite answer, are more difficult to evaluate."[2] However, the highest levels are very appropriate for prayer because they provide a model for stretching our minds to explore uncharted areas in our faith life. The following is a brief description of Bloom's taxonomy:

Knowledge is a simple recall of facts stated directly.

Comprehension is the capacity to understand at the inferential level, what is written between the lines.

Application occurs when information learned is applied to a new situation.

Analysis is the ability to break down new information into smaller parts and analyze it; to be able pick out its unique characteristics and compare it with other ideas.

Synthesis is the creation of something new and original from the acquired knowledge.

Evaluation is the ability to make a judgment about how that information can be of value in one's own life situation.

Prayer: Choose a reading from Scripture or from a spiritual reading book, and walk through it, using the model above. The following are some specific questions to guide you through the process, but don't feel confined by the process. Your thoughts may lead you in totally new directions. It is your prayer. These sample questions are suggestions to help you get started.

What does the reading say?

What is the deeper meaning behind the words?

How can I apply the meaning in my own life?

How is the information in this reading similar to other things I have read in the Bible or other spiritual reading texts? How is it different?

How does this reading call me to a deeper relationship with God? What does it call me to do or to be?

What are the "God" values in this reading, and how does my life reflect these values? What are the characteristics of the problem?

It is possible to ask many other questions which can lead to deeper reflection on a reading. The following are some of the verbs that can be used at each level to develop one's own questions for reflection.

Knowledge *remember, recall, recognize, state, define, read, recite*

Comprehension *summarize, interpret, explain, organize describe in other words, classify*

Application *demonstrate, show, model, select, apply, explain*

Analysis *distinguish, chart, plan, contrast, compare, conclude, separate, show cause for, differentiate*

Synthesis *create, tell, make, compose, build, invent, develop, design, blend, imagine*

Evaluation *choose, judge, decide, verify, evaluate, value, select*

---

[1] Bloom, Benjamin. *Taxonomy of Educational Objectives*. David McKay Company, Inc. 1956.

[2] Carlile, Vowery Dodd. *Multicultural Legends and Folktales*. Educational Impressions, 1995.

Sacred geometry

"So Pythagoras knew what he was doing when he gave that subject of geometry to the world. He knew that ultimately the lovers of truth and the true devotees would pass through it into the higher exaltation of the soul. His esoteric teachings did not live on, but his geometry was like the parables of Christ. Hidden in it are the sacred mysteries."

—Elizabeth Clare Prophet

The world is full of geometry—circles, squares, rectangles, triangles, ovals…Hidden within every plant, every flower, the sun and moon, and the clouds and stars are sacred mysteries.

Prayer: Take a walk today or look out the window to notice evidence of God's sacred geometry. Choose one object, and focus on the individual shapes. Do you see the circles and triangles? Do you see the rectangular shapes and ovals? Does the object have four sides, five sides, or more? Is it a pentagon, a hexagon, or an octagon?

Thank God for the simplicity of shapes and for the simplicity of life. Say yes to God's invitation to enter the sacred circle.

Plato tells us that

"God ever geometrizes,"

and Galileo says that

"The universe. . .cannot be read until we have learned the language and we have become familiar with the characters in which it is written. It is written in mathematical language, and the letters are triangles, circles, and other geometrical figures, without which means it is humanly impossible to comprehend a single word."

Learn to read the language of the universe today.

Sacred geometry two

"Mighty is geometry; joined with art, resistless."

—Euripides

Infinity is an abstraction because it is beyond our comprehension. It is a concept, an idea that reaches beyond the confines of our ability to reason and even beyond our capacity to imagine. God is infinite. Acknowledging our inability to understand is the first step toward opening ourselves to the possibility of knowing a truth beyond ourselves.

Geometric shapes and forms can lead to deeper truths not because they are complex, but because they are the epitome of simplicity. All of matter can be reduced to geometry. Johannes Kepler tells us that "Where there is matter, there is geometry."

Lines, circles, squares, and pentagons...what do they tell us of God? Is it that when we reduce all things to basic shapes, we allow ourselves to move from the complex to the simple and therein find God who is infinite simplicity?

Prayer: Cut out a variety of geometric forms (such as a circle, a straight line, a square, a pentagon, an oval, a rhombus, a rectangle, and a hexagon), and put them in an envelope. Choose one form during a prayer period, and allow yourself to simply focus on that form. Ask a few of the following questions to guide your reflections:

How is God like this shape?

What are the characteristics of this shape?

What can I learn about God from this shape?

What does this shape have to teach me?

What role does this shape play in my life?

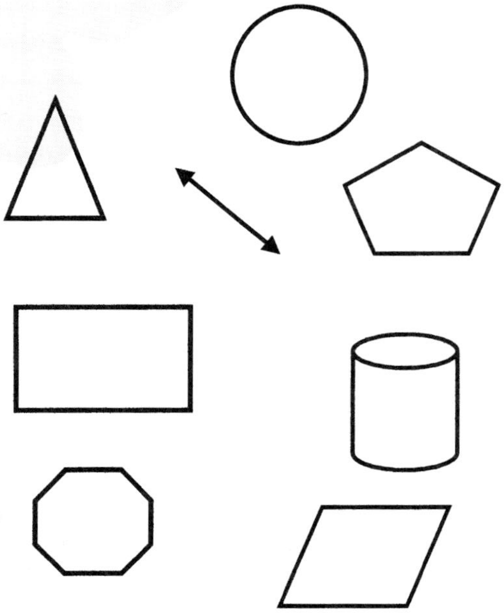

A potpourri of math/logic ideas for prayer

Make a Time Line

Choose a person in Scripture or a saint or holy person, and make a time line of his or her faith journey by jotting down important actions and events known about him or her. As you make your time line, look for ways in which it parallels your own faith journey.

Prayer: Ask for the gift of openness to change. Let the Spirit guide you through the examples of holy and wise people and call you to deeper holiness and union with God.

Evaluate the Problem & Make a Plan

All of us desire to grow and become better than we are. Sometimes, however, the task seems almost overwhelming. This prayer invites us to take steps toward the changes we would like to see in our lives.

Prayer: Choose one thing about your life you would like to change. It may be a negative habit or a relationship that needs healing. Be honest with yourself about the problem, and design a step-by-step plan to do something about it. Ask God for the gift of perseverance to follow through on your plan.

The Observation Prayer

God's love and presence surrounds us, but sometimes we are too busy to see it. At other times, we let negative thinking cloud our ability to notice the good things God has done.

Prayer: set aside 15 minutes to notice the good things around you. Look for beauty in everyday things and acts of kindness. Then thank God for enabling you to share in the Divine Presence.

The Addition Prayer

Humans always seem to want more—more possessions, more wealth, more power. We believe that the more we have the happier we will be. Yet in the deepest core of our being when we allow ourselves to listen, we know that the acquisition of things does not bring happiness. The addition prayer invites us to acquire new insights or new ways of doing things that will enrich our spiritual life. What can you add to your life to make it more fulfilling?

Prayer: Think of a characteristic of the Christian life such as patience, honesty, generosity, kindness, or self-control. Ask God to help you add that characteristic to your life today.

The Subtraction Prayer

We all do things we later regret. Sometimes it's a harsh word or a moment of insensitivity to another's needs. Many things we do each day pull us away from God. The subtraction prayer invites us to analyze the traits and characteristics that distance us from God and consciously seek to subtract them from our lives.

Prayer: Look back at the events of a single day. Is there a pattern of negativity that continues to recur? Do you lose your temper quickly? Do you yell when upset? Do you continually tell others (by words or actions) you are too busy to listen to them? Choose one action that keeps you from living fully in love and service to others, and consciously strive to subtract it at least once the following day.

Triangle Poem

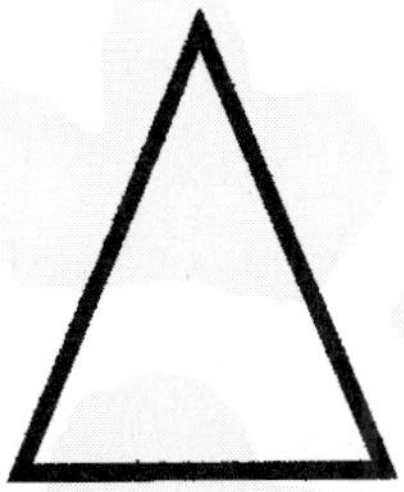

A triangle poem has three sides. Use the model of a triangle poem to capture a spiritual truth or insight.

Prayer: Ask God for the openness to listen and respond and to move from passivity to activity in God's name. Use the triangle above to write down words or phrases you would like to remember from your prayer, and allow them to guide you through the day as you recall God's voice in your life. There is no predetermined starting or ending point; any line can be the first or last.

The Cause-and-Effect Prayer

For every action in life there is a reaction. For every cause there is an effect. The cause-and-effect prayer provides an avenue to understand why some actions make us feel good and others do not.

Prayer: Take some time during the course of a day to reflect on your actions during the past several hours. What actions do you feel really good about? What actions do you regret because of their negative effects? Ask God to give you the insight to see the effects of your actions and the courage to choose those actions that will bring peace to your life and the lives of those around you.

Chapter two resources

Books

Bloom, Benjamin. *Taxonomy of Educational Objectives*. David McKay Company, Inc., 1956.

Carlile, Vowery Dodd. *Multicultural Legends and Tales*. Educational Impressions, 1995.

Cunningham, Beverly. *Quick Thinking: Critical and Creative Thinking Challenges*. ECS Learning Systems, 1995.

Ritter, Darlene. *Math Art*. Creative Teaching Press, 1995.

Vogt, Sharon. *Multicultural Math*. Frank Shaffer Publications, Inc., 1995.

Zaslavsky, Claudia. *Multicultural Math: Hands-On Math Activities from Around the World*. Scholastic Professional Books, 1996.

Electronic Sources

http://www.angelfire.com/biz/DynoWomyn/logmath.html

http://www.cookps.act.edu.au/mi_logic.htm

http://www.education.com/teachspace/intelligences/logical.jsp

http://ivc.uidaho.edu/flbrain/mathematical.htm

http:www.multi-intell.com/mi_background/lm.htm

http://www.newcityschool.org/innovations/mi/logicalmathematic.html

Finding God through the creative arts

CHAPTER THREE

"Creativity is . . . seeing something that doesn't exist already. You need to find out how you can bring it into being and [in] that way be a playmate with God."

—Michele Shea

Finding God through creative arts

Michelangelo, Leonardo da Vinci, the great stained glass artists of the past and present, the European grandmother who hand-stitched an altar cloth, the African tribesman who carved an image of Jesus, the Russian who created an icon to praise God . . . these people and many thousands of others throughout time and history have known the power of prayer through creating.

The visual-spatial learners are those who learn best through the creative arts—through painting, sculpting, and drawing. Their imaginations are fertile, and they can see what others do not. Their ability is the capacity to see beyond the reality in front of them and to create new models and new ways of being in greater harmony with the universe.

For these learners, prayer is colorful and fanciful. It does not follow a routine. It has multiple forms and shapes. The Sacred is found in beauty and invites the pray-er to be a co-creator and to add new dimensions to reality that reveal anew the hand of the Master Artist at work.

These learners come to know God through participating in prayer with paint and brush, pencil and crayon, fabric and dye, charcoal and pastel. The opportunity to create is a prayer for the visual-spatial learner. They find God easily in beautiful settings filled with color, whether at the beach, in a personal sacred space, or in a magnificent cathedral.

They see God as a messy God covered with paint, a laughing God delighting in creating, an artist, a dreamer. They feel called to the artist's studio to play with the artist's tools that they might come to know God the Artist more deeply.

New pathways to God are opened through creativity. The visually-spatially gifted know this in the deepest recesses of their beings. It is in and through the act of creating that they are transformed.

Mandalas

"...the power of the world always works in circles, and everything tries to be round.
The wind, in its greatest power, whirls. Birds make their nests in circles...
the sun comes forth and goes down in a circle..."

—Black Elk, Oglala Dakota Elder

Mandala means "circle" in the Sanskrit language. In art, the term mandala refers to a symbol that is done in any medium in a circular format. The idea of drawing mandalas for religious purposes goes back thousands of years and can be traced to cultures as diverse as the Buddhists of Tibet and the Navajo of North America.

Mandalas symbolize wholeness and always originate at a center. The creation of a mandala draws one toward the center of one's being while, at the same time, showing how all of life is interconnected. All religious traditions teach about the reality of an inner center within all beings—a center from which flows the energy that nurtures and sustains life. All religions stress the importance of getting in touch with this center as a means of deepening the spiritual life. This spiritual life is developed from within and then radiates outward to encompass ever widening circles of reality.

The mandala is an art form, but it is also a form of prayer. From the center of a mandala, a symmetrical pattern radiates outward visually illustrating how all is connected. The drawing of a mandala can be a prayerful experience in and of itself, as the lines and colors blend to form patterns in life. The mandala provides an avenue that enables us to move from our cognitive, rational thought patterns to an expanded awareness by tapping into our imaginations.

Prayer: Draw several concentric circles. In the center circle draw an object or symbol that is important in your life right now. Complete the mandala by drawing designs using different colors and shapes to form patterns in the outlying circles. There is no right or wrong way to draw a mandala. Each will be a unique expression of your inner self at a specific point in time. Once you have finished, sit quietly and reflect on the significance of what you have drawn.

Sample of mandalas

A prayer quilt

Various cultures throughout the world have celebrated the art of quilting. Traditional quilts are made from scraps of cloth stitched together, but they may also be made from a variety of materials. Cloth quilts are used for warmth and comfort on cold days, and most quilts are symbols of remembrance. Within the creativity of the quilt, stories are often woven to pass down from generation to generation the history of a family, a time, or a place.

A prayer quilt can be stitched of cloth in the traditional manner, but for those who do not sew but appreciate the beauty of the quilt, there is an alternate way.

Prayer: Cut several squares of poster board 9" x 9". Draw a diamond shape on each of the squares. Within each diamond shape, draw, paint, or use a computer image or other medium to illustrate a theme you want to include in your prayer. For example, the image in a gratitude quilt should represent things in your life for which you are grateful. The images in a hope quilt should represent things for which you dream—things that give meaning and direction to your life. You can also make a prayer-in-progress.

Proverbs in pictures

A love of the land and an unquestioned acceptance of the responsibility of caring for the Great Spirit's creation is a hallmark of Native American spirituality. Their proverbs can serve as a source of prayer by inviting us to recognize God's presence in our lives.

Prayer: Choose one of the proverbs below to illustrate. Reflect on the words as you use any artistic media to create a picture to represent the wisdom contained therein.

"With all things and in all things, we are relatives."

—Sioux

"Stand in the light when you want to speak out."

—Crow

"We are all one child spinning through Mother Sky."

—Shawnee

"Sin is not allowed in God's tepee."

—Mohawk

"When we show our respect for other living things, they respond with respect for us."

—Arapaho

"We should be as water, which is lower than all things yet stronger even than the rocks."

—Sioux

"Everything the Power does, it does in a circle."

—Lakota

"The greatest strength is gentleness."

—Iroquois

"Every fire is the same size when it starts."

—Seneca

"The frog does not drink up the pond in which it lives."

—Sioux

"Wisdom comes only when you stop looking for it and start living the life the Creator intended for you."

—Hopi

"All plants are our brothers and sisters. They talk to us and if we listen, we can hear them."

—Arapaho

"God gives us each a song."

—Ute

"When you lose the rhythm of the drumbeat of God, you are lost from the peace and rhythm of life."

—Cheyenne

Creative journal activities

"I found I could say things with color and shapes that I couldn't say in any other way—things that I had no words for."

—Georgia O'Keeffe

Prayer: Choose one of the following, and enjoy being creative with the Master Artist.

Draw a symbol to represent your relationship with God.

Create an abstract design with colors that reflect how you are feeling right now.

Draw a picture of the animal you would most like to be.

Create an abstract pattern that reflects an emotion—hope, joy, sadness, love, hurt, anxiety.

Draw a picture of yourself doing something you never imagined you would.

Celebrate creativity with colors.

Sketch a scene a day of all that you are seeing, and give thanks.

Put a photo in your journal.

Design a picture that starts with your thumbprint.

Create a maze.
Make a picture of what you think love looks like.

Make a picture to represent what you think God looks like.

Design a holy card.

Choose a scene from Scripture, and illustrate it.

Illustrate a favorite prayer.

Create a border around a haiku you have written.

What color is God?

What color is life?

Cut out geometric shapes and create a shape prayer.

Border art

Prayer: Be creative with poetry, proverbs, Scripture passages, or quotations. Write out the words, and frame them with border art. Put the finished product in a place where it provides both beauty and food for thought.

Flow chart prayer

Prayer: Trace your emotions through the course of a day, a week, or a month. Use colors, designs and/or pictures to express the different emotions you feel. Reflect on what was happening when the emotions were positive and what was happening when they were negative. In what ways did you feel God's presence? Use your flow chart to write a prayer as a tool for gaining self-understanding.

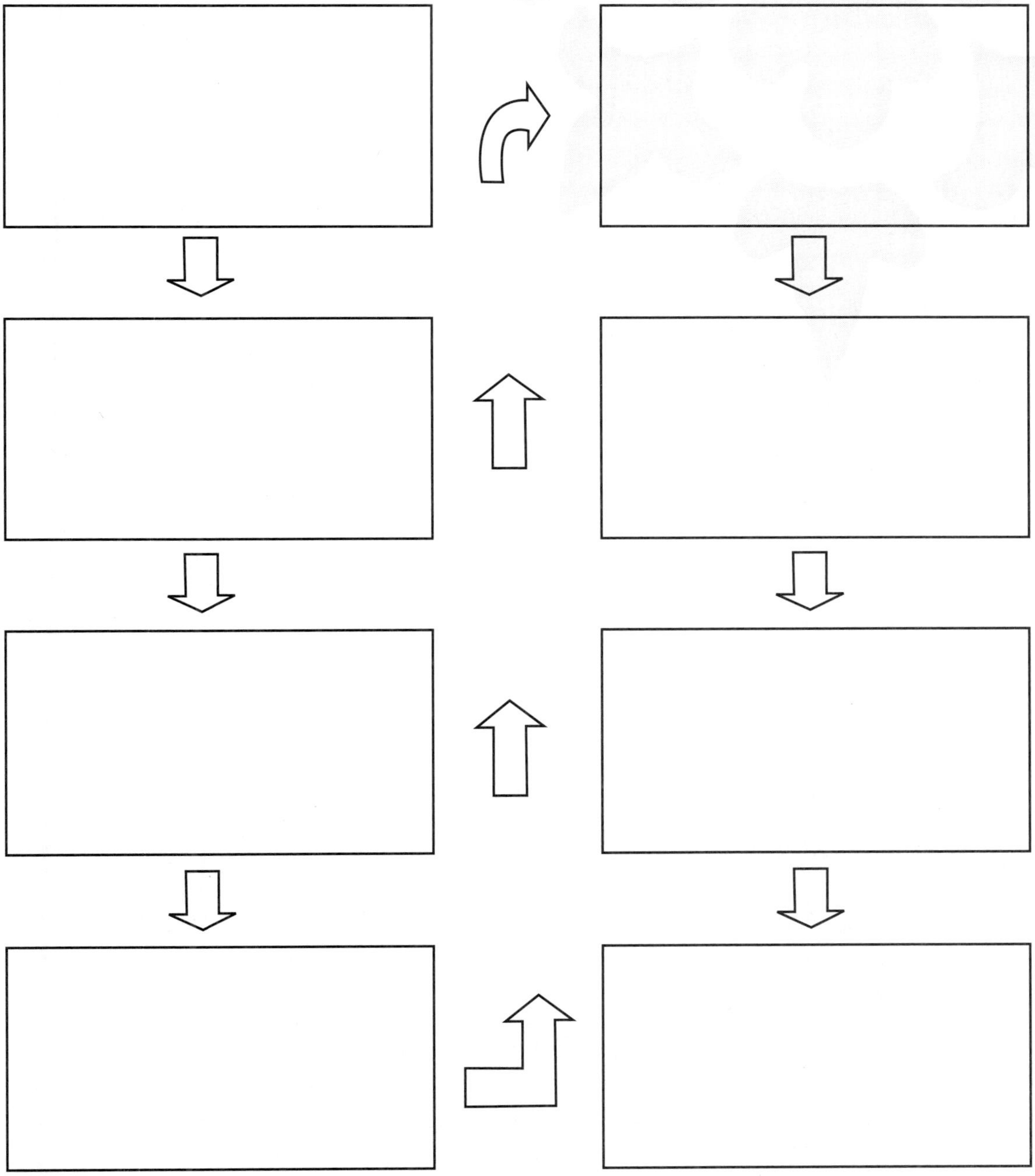

Mola prayers

The *mola* is a type of folk art from the San Blas Islands, near Panama, that is made by cutting and sewing fabric designs through several layers of fabric to produce a multicolored pattern or picture. The Kuna Indians sew molas onto blouses; in fact, mola means "blouse" in the Kuna language. The concept of the mola can be extended to art designs that involve several layers of colors representing a single image. Although traditionally done with fabric, the molas can also be done by layering colored paper.

Prayer: Choose a single object that speaks to you of God's creativity. Make a simple outline of the object onto a sheet of paper of a primary color (red, blue, or yellow). Cut out the shape, and glue it onto a sheet of paper of a secondary color (such as green). Cut around the outline, but leave a border of approximately 1/4" all around. Glue the shapes onto a sheet of dark-colored paper. Cut around the outline again, still maintaining a 1/4" border. Glue the shapes onto white paper, and follow the cutting and gluing procedure again. Glue the shapes onto a black sheet of paper. Then cut narrow tube-like shapes of assorted colors from your scraps and glue them onto the background paper around your primary object.

Thank God for the beauty this object has brought into your life, and reflect on how you are called to bring beauty into the lives of others.

The cross of liberation and hope

The cross is central to our worship as Christians. It is prominently displayed in every church and in our homes. The people of El Salvador use the cross as an expression of their faith and hope in the midst of suffering by depicting on the cross itself images that give meaning to their everyday lives—the sun, land, animals, family, home, etc. Their crosses reflect where God is present to them in their struggles. The brightness of the colors used also give evidence of their belief that through the cross the future will be better.

Prayer: Create a cross, or use the outline on the following page, that incorporates the symbols of your life. Choose photos, magazine pictures, cards, small objects and anything else that will enable you to design a cross that reflects your reality. Use crayons, markers, paint or any other medium to join your objects together. Hang your cross where you will see it often and give thanks for the many blessings in your life.

The cross of ________________

Guided imagery

The capacity to imagine is a hallmark of the visual-spatial intelligence. Prayer using guided imagery is especially fruitful since it allows the spirit to wander into new and uncharted territory within the mind.

Prayer: Find a spot that is comfortable for you, and take a deep breath. Imagine yourself being lifted up and gently placed on a cloud. Relax. Almost imperceptibly the cloud begins to move. You feel very secure, however, and are not afraid. You peek over the side and notice that your home is now a speck in the distance. You look directly below and notice that you have crossed into another place. The view from above is quite beautiful. Allow yourself to simply enjoy it for a while.

Eventually your cloud is no longer over the land but out over the ocean. It is a phenomenal sight from above. The water is a million shades of blues and greens and browns. There is so much of it. It seems to go on forever. Suddenly, the absolute stillness which has surrounded you is broken by a voice, seemingly from nowhere. The voice startles you but does not frighten you because you know it is God speaking to you. The voice tells you about the beauty and grandeur of what you see. You feel God's reassuring voice reach into your heart. Listen to the voice and spend a while pondering what you hear.

God now shows you the oceans teeming with fish. Then you see a beautiful coastline in the distance. As you draw closer, you see birds soaring through the crystal clear air, and fruits and vegetables growing in abundance everywhere. Take a moment to feel God present to you in the beauty of what you see.

God leads you farther along the coast but now you see oil slicks lapping at the shores. Moving more inland, the terrain looks denuded. Everything is brown and dry. The dust rising off the sides of the deforested mountains makes it difficult to see anything else. You begin to notice the landscape littered with trash and encampments dotting the mountainsides. God leads you closer to the Earth and you begin to see the people clearly. There are millions of them all huddled together clinging to life on the edges of the cities. You begin to sense their need and suffering. You feel the interconnectedness of God's people and creation—and you feel the loss of people starving, animals dying, and plant life lost forever.

You are troubled by what you see, but at the same time you feel held in God's loving embrace. You know it is safe to ask God about what you see, so you begin to speak to God. You ask God "what happened, how did it get this way?"

What does God tell you? You spend quite a while with God—sometimes asking questions, sometimes listening, and sometimes just sitting together quietly feeling God's presence.

As you talk to God, you feel more and more connected to God's creation. You begin to feel yourself slowly moving back toward where you are sitting. God's voice fades, but you still feel connected. As you gradually become more aware of the room where you sit, spend some time feeling and reflecting on your connection to all creation.

A potpourri of creative art ideas for prayer

Tissue-Paper Prayer

Rip some shapes from different colors of tissue paper. Put some water-based sealer or glue and water in a container. Glue the tissue paper onto white paper or cardboard. Brush directly on top of the tissue paper. Overlap some of the pieces.

Prayer: As the new colors, shapes and forms emerge, thank God for the gift of creativity. Take joy in the moment of creating something new. Hear God's call to you to continue to co-create the world so that it reflects the Divine Image.

Batik Prayer

Batik is an ancient art form found throughout the world. Africa is especially renowned for the beautiful batiks that come from many countries on the continent. Batik is essentially a resist technique that is done on cloth with wax and dye. However, it is possible to simulate batik designs by using wax crayons and watercolor paints.

Prayer: Use crayons to draw a design or scene on a plain sheet of typing paper. Press hard with the crayons so that the colors are bright. Then brush over the entire painting with a single color of a light to moderate color of watercolor paint. The paint will adhere to white spaces but be resisted by the wax in the crayon. Gently take the wet sheet and crumble it in your hand. Carefully open it and lay it between two sheets of newspaper. Iron the top sheet of the newspaper on a moderate setting. Remove your picture, and you will have a beautiful batik.

Thank God for the gifts of art that come to us from many cultures. Look at the beauty of your creation, and give thanks to God the Artist, who created a world filled with wonders. Take time to look at the beauty in your world today.

Praying with Pastels

Chalk pastels are very soft and smudge easily. This quality allows for unique effects by mixing and blending different colors. Try mixing colors on your paper by doing different types of strokes on top of the other or experiment with putting different colors on top of the other. Blend different colors using your fingers or a tissue. Draw with the pointed end of the pastel, and then try using the side for a different effect. Break the colors up by drawing lots of short strokes in one color around a central point.

Prayer: Take a sheet of white or colored paper, preferably a type of paper that has a slight texture. Allow your mind to relax as your hand makes designs on the paper. Choose colors that reflect your feelings at the moment. Don't worry about creating a perfect piece of art. Simply enter into the colors and designs, and go with the flow.

How does God invite you to enter into the colors and designs of the universe? Do you feel yourself being caught up in the swirling cosmos as your hand moves across the paper?

Salt Painting Prayer

> *"You are the salt of the earth; but if salt has lost its taste, how can its saltiness be restored? It is no longer good for anything, but is thrown out and trampled under foot."*
>
> -Matthew 5:13

When salt is sprinkled onto watercolor paint, the salt soaks up the color and leaves a grainy effect when the painting dries.

Prayer: Paint an object or scene with watercolors. Before the paint has dried, sprinkle lots of salt all over the paper. As the painting dries, it will soak up the salt. Shake off the excess salt when the painting is dry. The remaining salt will give the painting a sandy, textured effect.

Use your painting to reflect on your call to be "salt of the earth." How do you bring "flavor" into the lives of others? What will you do today that will enhance the flavor of life for yourself? For your family? For your friends? For strangers?

Chapter three resources

Books

Brussat, Frederic and Mary Ann. *Spiritual Rx: Prescriptions for Living a Meaningful Life.* Hyperion Press, 2000.

Cameron, Julia. *The Artist's Way: A Spiritual Path to Higher Creativity.* J. P. Tarcher, 2002.

Cassou, Michelle and Stewart Cubley. *Life, Paint and Passion: Reclaiming the Magic of Spontaneous Expression.* J. P. Tarcher, 1996.

Gerding, Jeri. *Drawing to God: Art as Prayer, Prayer as Art.* Sorin Books, 2001.

Henry, Sandi. *Cut-Paper Play!* Williamson, 1997.

Watt, Fiona. *The Usborne Book of Art Ideas.* Usborne, 2000.

Zona, Guy A. *The Soul Would Have No Rainbow if the Eyes Had No Tears and Other Native American Proverbs.* Simon and Schuster, 1994.

Electronic Sources

http://www.mandalaproject.org

http://www.mandali.com

Finding God through music
CHAPTER FOUR

"The aim and final reason of all music should be nothing else but the glory of God and the refreshment of the spirit."

—J. S. Bach

Finding God through music

Ntenga, chigubhu, and ***darabuka*** drums of Africa, the European ***bouzouki, tambura, balalaika*** and ***bandoura*** stringed instruments, the ***p'ip'a*** stringed instrument of China, the ***zamponas*** panflutes of Bolivia, the ***ghunghura*** dancing bells of India, the ***sistrum*** metal-and-wire shakers of Zimbabwe, and the calabash gourd ***kass-kassa*** of Togo are only a few of the millions of instruments throughout the world used to give praise to God.

Voices are raised in song and prayer in Spanish, English, Vietnamese, Quechua, Aymara, Japanese, and thousands of other languages and dialects. Music crosses the cultural divide easily. Anthropologists have studied cultures that exist without the use of reading and writing, but no culture has ever been found that existed without music. It is a universal prayer.

The musical-rhythmic individual is the one to whom music speaks in a special way. In education Gloria J. Klester tells us that:

> *The brain processes . . . [some] information bit-by-bit with the bits converging at a single point. This is the kind of linear thinking typically used in language and science. It yields facts, conclusions and "right" answers. But the brain can also process many bits of information all at once, releasing the results in divergent directions. This sort of thinking—called "holistic"—leads to hypotheses, metaphors and ambiguity. It is basic to emotion, imagination and creativity.*[1]

Music can lead our prayer in multiple directions. It opens up new pathways and new ways of knowing God. It moves away from the linear to the holistic realm, where logic is not as important as understanding. Musical-rhythmic prayer invites the pray-er to a state in which feelings, emotion, and creativity are valued and can be expressed. A personal relationship with God is developed through listening to music, singing, and/or playing a musical instrument.

A musical autobiography

"Within music lies all the wonders and keys to the miracles of life—natural and spiritual. Music can facilitate the process of change and growth."

—Ted Andrews

A musical autobiography is the story of your relationship to God through music. It charts the major events in your life through song and sound. Make a time line of approximately ten events or times in your life that reflect both high and low points. Find a song or piece of instrumental music that reflects how you felt at each of those times.

A few ideas to think about:

A childhood recollection of a very happy time

A childhood recollection of a very sad time

A favorite birthday

A memorable learning experience

A graduation

A special time with family

A special time with friends

A vacation memory

A time when you felt close to God

A time when you felt distant from God

A time of great joy

A time of great loneliness

A Christmas experience

An experience of being loved

Prayer: Listen to the music with a prayerful spirit. How does it make you feel? What is the rhythm of your life? Talk to God about your feelings. Invite God to enter into the song your life is writing.

Drumming

"The drum is the Great Spirit's favorite instrument. That's why we were all given a heartbeat."
—Mano, Navajo Elder

Drums are a musical instrument that can be found in cultures throughout the world. They are used by Aboriginal peoples living nomadic existences deep in jungles, as well as by those living in skyscrapers in large cities. What is it about drums that give them their universal appeal?

One drummer tells us. . .

Drumming brings us closer to mother nature... it is deeply steeped in ritual and for many centuries the people of the land have kept sacred their traditions through it. The sacredness of the drum comes from our own bodies, our own heartbeats, our own pulse.

These insights help us to understand why the drum has played such a central role in the lives of early peoples, but also invite us to explore the role the drum might play in our own lives as a tool for deepening self-awareness. Some studies today indicate that almost 98 percent of all disease in our society is related to stress and drumming is emerging as the transformational tool of our time. "Drumming is among the best ways for us to reconnect with nature herself," another drummer writes. She continues, "...this is a language we all speak, the beat of our hearts and the beat of the drum commune us with nature and all people of the earth."

This desire to reconnect with our inner selves, to feel connected to someone greater than ourselves, connected to the rhythm of the universe, is at the heart of prayer. Ancient peoples, modern researchers, and practitioners invite us to explore the drum's power as a tool for prayer, personal healing, and global transformation.

Drumming for prayer does not require any special musical knowledge. The beauty of the drum is that it can be used by anyone at anytime without music lessons or classroom study. The message of some who practice this is:

Drumming does not require any special training or a language to communicate what to do. We all know how to drum from the earliest age...and from the earliest age we join with others in drumming to our own rhythms.

The value of drumming is also being recognized for its capacity to alter alpha brain-wave patterns. Alpha is a mental relaxation state and can lead us to deeper prayer and meditation.

Prayer: Try one of the following with any type of drum available:

Find a comfortable place, and sit in a relaxed position so that the drum feels natural. Close your eyes and listen quietly to your heartbeat. Slowly begin to beat the drum to the sound of your own heartbeat. Allow yourself to feel your connectedness with the Earth. Feel the rhythm of the universe within yourself. Feel your connectedness to the Author of all creation. Give thanks for the beauty of the world, for the beauty of your life.

Choose a drumming cassette or CD. Listen to the beat. Allow yourself to feel the beat within you. You may choose to simply listen or begin to beat your own drum to the rhythms you are hearing. Feel the peace that comes with being at one with God, Creator of the universe.

Drumming Resources

Gordon, David and Steven. *Sacred Earth Drums.* CD or cassette. Sequoia, 1994.

______________. *Sacred Spirit Drums.* CD or cassette. Sequoia, 1996.

______________. *Drum Medicine.* CD or cassette. Sequoia, 1999.

Keita, Mamady Ijalit. *African Drums.* CD. Master Sound/Continental, 2000.

Yoshida, Kiyoshi. *Asian Drums.* CD. Pacific Moon, 2000.

______________. *Asian Drums II.* CD. Pacific Moon, 2001.

Chanting

"[Chanting is] the music of the cosmic spheres and the natural expression of our own consciousness . . . it is an important tool used by people everywhere to heal their bodies, quiet their minds, and bring the sacred into their lives."

—Don Campbell

Chant is global in its appeal. It can be simple rhythmic patterns such as the chants of Native Americans and Africans to the beat of drums or incredibly complex rhythmic patterns such as those found in Bali. It can be the voices of monks raised in Gregorian chant to one long sustained note with no rhythm at all, as among the Buddhists of Tibet with the chanting of the sacred Sanskrit "om." Regardless of the type of chant, its primary purpose is to quiet the mind and open the heart to God.

Why chant? Robert Gass suggests:

We chant to join our voices to the voices of
countless seekers, worshipers, mystics, and
lovers of life, in every time and in every place,
who have shared in sacred song.
We chant to fill our hearts and fill our homes
with loving and peaceful vibrations of sound.
We chant because it's fun.
We chant to help the stress and freneticness of
our busy lives melt away.
We chant to spread our wings and let our soul
take flight.
We chant for the sheer joy of letting our
God-given voices sing out.
We chant for the heartful communion that we
feel with others when we come together in song.
We chant our prayers to God, so that our lives
may be graced by more intimate Presence of the
One known by so many names.[1]

Chant can have a direct effect on our energy levels and physical bodies. It has also proven to be a powerful tool throughout history for transforming consciousness. It can serve as a bridge between our everyday busyness and deeper levels of consciousness. Anyone can chant. It does not require any special preparation or training.

According to Alaskan wilderness teacher David LaChapelle, "Chanting outside transforms our relationship to natural systems—makes us a part of them. This is not a concept—you feel it! I discover landscapes living inside of me, even while I'm living into the external landscape in a deeper way."[2]

Sample chants from several traditions:

Listen to the salutation to the dawn,
Look to this day for it is life, the very life of life.
—Sanskrit chant

O Great Spirit whose voice I hear in the winds
and whose breath gives life to all the world…
—Native American chant

Be praised, my Lord, for all Your creations
and especially for Brother Son
Who makes the day bright and luminous.
—St. Francis

O God, creator of our land, our earth, the trees, the animals and humans; All is for your honor.
—Ashanti, West Africa[3]

---

[1] Gass, Robert with Kathleen Brehony. *Chanting: Discovering Spirit in Sound*. Broadway Books. 1999. p10.
[2] Ibid. p106.
[3] Gass, Robert with Kathleen Brehony. *Chanting: Discovering Spirit in Sound*. Broadway Books. 2000. p198-199.

Prayer: Choose a favorite prayer or Scripture passage to chant. It can be a very simple chant with a single note or more complex with rising and falling notes. Allow your voice to lift your spirit to the Lord. If you do not wish to chant yourself, choose a tape or CD with chants, and allow the rhythms to lift your heart in prayer.

Chanting Resources

Afghanistan: Chants des Pashai. CD. Le Chant Du Monde, 1991.

Ave Maria—Gregorian Chants. CD. New World Music, 1999.

Buddhist Chants and Peace Music. CD. Mci, 1999.

Chants of India. CD. Emd/Angel, 1997.

Classical Chants from Tunisia. CD. Al Sur, 1995.

Gregorian Chants. CD. Mci, 1999.

Mother Wisdom: Original and Traditional Chants. CD. Kiva, 2001.

Native Suite—Chants, Dances and the Remembered Earth. CD or cassette. Warner Bros. 1996.

Enchanted: The Best of Robert Gass & On Wings of Song. CD or cassette. Spring Hill, 1999.

Sacred Healing Chants of Tibet. CD. Eastwest, 1999.

Sacred Spirit: Chants and Dances of the Native Americans. CD or cassette. Virgin, 1998.

Synagogue Chants. CD. Le Chant Du Monde, 1998.

Psalms to songs

The psalms are lyrical poetry that express the passion of the different periods of history in which they were written. There are 150 psalms, the earliest of which date from the Exile. Others can be identified with the period after the return to Jerusalem. Some of the psalms also reflect the wisdom writings of later times, but others belong to the period of the kings. David is considered the author of many of the psalms.

The psalms were originally considered hymns of praise and were used in the liturgical worship of the Temple. Christians later adopted the psalms and incorporated them into the daily prayer of the Church. For the early Hebrews and later Christians, the psalms give voice to the individual and communal experience of God. While the psalms are still sung daily in monastic communities, this practice is not frequent in the daily lives of most Christians. Recapturing the lyrical and poetic beauty of the psalms through song can deepen our understanding of their meaning and lead us to see new insights.

Prayer: Try one of the following:

Choose a psalm and put it to music. It can be a simple chant, a paraphrase of Scripture sung to a tune you already know, or a more complex musical composition.

A number of musicians have put the psalms to music and recorded them professionally. Choose one, and listen to the words and melody as you join your prayer to that of the ancient psalmists.

Abey and Swapna. Anoint Me—Praise and Worship with the Psalms. CD. Orchard, 2000.
Friedman, Joe. Songs from the Psalms. CD. Orchard, 2000.
Singing the Psalms, Volumes 1–5. CD or cassette. OCP.
Willcock, Christopher. Psalms for the Journey. CD or cassette. OCP.
____________. Psalms for Feasts and Seasons. cassette. OCP.

Choose a psalm, and read it prayerfully while listening to background instrumental music.

Psalm Websites

http://www.homestead.com/metricalpsalms/

This site has a number of metrical psalms, which are psalms written in a metered, poetic format that enables them to be set to familiar hymn tunes.

http://www.dsj.org/prayer/psalms.htm

This website by the Diocese of San Jose, California, has organized the psalms according to special needs.

http://www.geocities.com/Heartland/Pond/9117/

The Psalms Place is a multifaceted Christian website that is based upon the Psalms of David. It includes music, commentary, poetry, and even trivia on the psalms.

www.bluecloud.org/psalms.html

This site provides an opportunity to pray the psalms daily with the Monks Canticle Collection.

www.christdesert.org/noframes/chant/psalmton.html

This website provides information on the chanting of the psalms.
This site provides musical accompaniment to an extensive number of the psalms.

www.beliefnet.com/author/author_65.html

This web page by columnist Cynthia Bourgeault offers insight and instructions on singing the psalms.

Musical journaling

"The colorful, often emotion-laden world of music and imagery provides a window to view our inner selves. Through turning our senses inward, the imagination, stirred by fine music, enables us to view our feelings, memories, and intuitions."

—Carol A. Bush

Music invites us to enter a sacred space within ourselves. It provides a source of calmness and helps us to slow down and get in touch with our inner rhythms.

The Australian Aborigines believe that:

> *Music influences all humankind, and, indeed, the energy of music can be healing for both the body and the planet. Listening to peaceful music set to the pace of the human pulse can have a profound positive influence on one's nerves and mental state. Everyone is musical and is influenced by it. It is the voice of our planet communicating to the universe.*[1]

Leading scientists and physicians today are recognizing that the body, mind, spirit connection is more than just a well-oiled machine. Fritj of Capra, a quantum physicist, and Deepak Chopra, a physician, both agree that the human body is more music than machine, that there are rhythms of the human body that cannot be quantified or predicted.

Journaling with music can lead to a greater harmony with inner rhythms. It can create that sacred space where feelings, emotions, and intuition are valued and where new insights emerge that can bring clarity to situations and events in life. Music integrates head-talk and heart-talk. It provides another lens to view reality.

Prayer: Find a quiet place where you will not be disturbed. Choose a music CD or cassette with instrumental music. Close your eyes and listen to the music. It is often helpful to begin this prayer with a focus question that reflects a current issue in your life. Allow your imagination to flow with the rhythm of the music. When you have finished listening to the music, jot down your thoughts in a journal. What insights did you gain from the music? Do you see the issue with more clarity? What is your heart telling you?

A variation on this prayer is to journal with crayons, colored pencils, or pastels. Allow your hand to move with the music. Choose colors that reflect the music for you. Drawings can also lead to new insights. What do the colors, shapes, or design that you drew reveal to you? How does your musical art lend clarity to your focus question?

Stephanie Merritt offers some excellent musical selections for this type of prayer.[2]

Music for Solitude and Introspection

J.S. Bach	*Jesu, Joy of Man's Desiring* Cello Suites *Air on the G String*
Barber	*Adagio for Strings*
Beethoven	Piano Sonatas
Chopin	*The Meditative Chopin* by Roy Eaton
Debussy	*Clair de Lune*
Franck	Symphony in D minor
Rachmaninoff	Piano Concerto Nos. 2 and 3
J.S. Bach	*Sheep May Safely Graze*

Music for Meditation

Beethoven	Symphony No. 9 (3rd movement) Piano Concerto No. 3 (2nd movement) Violin Concerto (2nd movement)
Brahms	Violin Concerto (2nd movement)
Dvorak	Cello Concerto (2nd movement) Symphony No. 9 "From the New World"
Franck	*Panis Angelicus*
Mahler	Symphony No. 4 (3rd movement) Symphony No. 7 (2nd movement)
Schubert	*Ave Maria*

[1] Morgan, Marlo. *Message from Forever*. Cliff Street Books/HarperCollins Publishers, 1998. p. 317.

[2] Merritt, Stephanie. *Mind, Music & Imagery*. Aslan Publishing, 1996. pp. 150–152.

Pray with music from around the world

"Music is the vernacular of the human soul."

—Geoffrey Latham

The words of Sir Frederick Doyle spoken in 1948—"Once a photograph of the earth, taken from the outside, is available…a new idea as powerful as any in history will let loose"—are a powerful reminder of the visual we now have that shows the interconnectedness of all life on earth. Pick up the newspaper, listen to the radio, or watch the evening news. It is impossible not to know of the realities of the AIDS epidemic throughout the African continent, the destruction of the South American rainforest, the earthquakes in India, the typhoons in the Philippines, the hurricanes that hit the Caribbean, and the religious wars and acts of terrorism throughout the world.

Our faith is tested by the negativity which surrounds us. Where is God in all of this? How can a loving God allow this to happen? But in the midst of the fear is also a call—a call to move outside of our comfort zones and see ourselves as a part of this suffering humanity; a call to recognize our brothers and sisters in the poor and marginalized; a call to connect with our Muslim and Jewish and Buddhist brothers and sisters; a call to connect with our indigenous brothers and sisters who have not forgotten that all of life is connected.

Prayer: Choose a country or place in the world that you would like to pray for, and find a piece of music from there. Choose a comfortable spot in which to sit. Light a candle. Close your eyes and listen to the music. Allow yourself to feel your connection to the people and the land that the music represents. Pray for them. Join your prayer with their prayer for a world in which all may live in peace and harmony. Feel the peace that comes with understanding.

Bibliography of World Music

Africa

Colors of the World: Africa. CD. Allegro Music, 2000.

Festival Africa! CD. Compass, 2001.

Tribal Chants, Drums and Songs of Africa. CD. Legacy, 1995.

Voices of Africa. CD. Brentwood, 2000.

Sam Fan Thomas. Makassi (Cameroon). CD. Terrascape, 1998.

Kora Melodies: Music from Gambia, West Africa. CD. Rounder Select, 1992.

Tarabu: Music from the Swahili of Kenya. CD. Shanachie, 1997.

Under the Moroccan Sky. CD. Sounds True, 2001.

Music of Tanzania. CD. World Music Library. 1994.

Ancient Wisdom: Songs and Fables from Zimbabwe. CD. Latitudes, 1998.

Asia & the South Pacific

Air Mail Music: Afghanistan. Playasound, 2000.

Asian Journey. CD. Metacom, 1998.

Buddhist Chants: Harmony of the Soul. CD. Essex Entertainment, 1995.

Music from Cambodia and Vietnam. CD. Arc, 2000.

Music from the Oasis Towns of Central Asia. CD. Globe Style, 2000.

The Music of China. CD. Retro Music, 1995.

Chinese Lullabies. CD. Wind Records, 1996.

Colors of the World: Fiji. CD. Allegro, 1999.

Songs from India. CD. Eclipse Music Group, 1999.

India. CD. Mastertone, 1998.

Shalom Israel: Hava Nagila. CD. Discom, 1998.

Iranian Classical Traditions. CD. Musique d'Abord, 1997.

The Music of Japan. CD. Retro Music, 1995.

All the Best from Japan: Popular Kyoto Melodies. CD. Madacy, 1994.

Traditional Music from Central Java. CD. Nimbus, 1998.

A Taste of Asia: Laos/Thailand/China. CD. Nimbus, 1995.

Songs from the Middle East. CD. Eclipse Music Group, 1999.

Air Mail Music: Myanmar. CD. Playasound, 1999.

Native Music of Nepal. CD. Legacy, 1997.

Greetings from the Philippines. CD. Pmf Music, 1997.

A World of Music: Russia. CD. St. Clair Entertainment Group, 2000.

Sacred Songs of Russia. CD. Paraclete Press, 1999.

Music of the South Pacific. CD. Master Sound, 2001.

A World of Music: Tibet. CD. St. Clair Entertainment Group, 2000.

Zen Garden. CD. Avalon Music, 2000.

Australia, New Zealand, & New Guinea

Songs of Australia. CD. Direct Source. 2000.

I Call Australia Home. CD. Celestial Harmonies, 2000.

Spirit of Uluru: Music of Australian Aborigines. CD. Laserlight, 1998.

Windim Mambu: Sacred Flute Music from New Guinea. CD. Rounder Select, 1999.

Maori Songs of New Zealand. CD. Delta Music, 1998.

Rainbow Serpent: Music for Didgeridoo and Percussion. CD. Celestial Harmonies, 1994.

Europe

Balkan Memories. CD. Discom, 1998.

Patterson, William. *Seascapes: Celtic Inspirations.* CD. Columbia River Entertainment Group, 1997.

A World of Music: France. CD. St. Clair Entertainment Group, 2000.

A World of Music: Germany. CD. St. Clair Entertainment Group, 2000.

Music of Greece. CD. Anodyne Records, 2000.

Traditional Songs and Dances of Hungary. CD. Legacy, 1999.

James, Michael et al. *Dánta Dé: Classic Sacred Music of Ireland.* CD. Ave Maria Press, 1996.

Italian Music Odyssey. CD. Putumayo, 2000.

Soul of Poland. CD. Madacy, 1996.

Fados and Folksongs from Portugal. CD. Delta, 1998.

A World of Music: Scotland. CD. St. Clair Entertainment Group, 2000.

Wintersongs: Winter Holiday in Sweden. CD. Northside Records, 2001.

North America & the Caribbean

Kenoly, Ron. *Lift Him Up. (African American)* CD. Integrity Music, Inc., 1992.

Song of the Hills: Instrumental Impressions of Appalachian Classics. CD. Shanachie, 1999.

Caribbean Celebration. CD. Musical Reflections, 1998.

Music of the Caribbean. CD. Intersound, 1995.

Ho Lung, Richard M.O.P. and Friends. *I Will Serve You (Caribbean).* CD. OCP, 1999.

Ho Lung, Richard M.O.P. and Friends. *Working for the Lord (Caribbean).* CD. OCP, 1999.

Music of Cuba. CD. A World of Music, 1997.

Air Mail Music: Haiti. CD. Playasound, 1999.

Ata, Damasco. *From the Valley to the Throne: Gospel Hymns of Hawaii.* CD. Ululoa Productions, 2000.

Haugen, Marty et al. *Spirit of Malia (Music from Hawaii).* CD. GIA Publications, 1999.

Martinique. CD. Bci Music, 1998.

Authentic Native American Music. CD. Delta Music, 1995.

Native Song. CD. Metacom, 1999.

Tribal Winds: Music from Native American Flutes. CD. EarthBeat!, 1996.

Tribal Waters: Music from Native Americans. CD. EarthBeat!, 1998.

Weaving the Strands: Music by Contemporary Native American Women. CD. Red Feather Music, 1998.

Ballads, Banjo Tunes, and Sacred Songs of Western North Carolina. CD. Smithsonian Folkways, 1996.

South America, Central America & Mexico

A World of Music: The Andes. CD. St. Clair Entertainment Group, 2000.

Spirit of Brazil: Songs of Amazon Indians. CD. Pmf Music Factory, 1998.

The Music of Brazilia. CD. Passport International Music, 1995.

International Flavors: Colombia. CD. St. Clair Entertainment Group, 1998.

Marimba de Guatemala. CD. A World of Music, 1997.

Traditional Music of the Incas. Legacy, 1995.

Putumayo Presents: Mexico. CD. Putumayo, 2001.

Traditional Music from Panama. CD. Nimbus, 1999.

Cortés, Eleazar. *Somos la Iglesia.* CD. OCP, 1997.

General

Music from the Coffee Lands. CD. Putumayo, 1997.

Colors of the World: Music from the Four Corners. CD. Allegro, 1997.

Putumayo Presents: Gardens of Eden. CD. Putumayo, 2001.

Global Meditation: Authentic Music from Meditative Traditions of the World. CD. Ellipsis Arts, 1994.

Youngblood, Mary. *Heart of the World.* CD. Silver Wave, 1999.

Hysom, Dennis and Dan Alvarez. *In Joyful Harmony.* CD. Discovery Channel Store, 1998.

Manibusan, Jesse. *Misa del Mundo (Music from Encuentro 2000).* CD. OCP, 1999.

Native Wisdom: World Music of the Spirit. CD. Narada, 1996.

Alfano, Jorge. *One Heart.* Lyrichord, 1997.

Prayer: A Multi-Cultural Journey of the Spirit. CD. Soundings of the Planet, 1998.

Music from the Tea Lands. CD. Putumayo, 2000.

A potpourri of music ideas for prayer

Rhythm Instruments

People throughout the world have made music since the beginning of time. The earliest people probably made music by clapping their hands, stamping their feet and, of course, using their voices. Sticks, tree bark, stones, seeds, animal skins...all have been used to make musical instruments. Wood on wood, stone on stone, wood on stone, and seeds within a gourd all produce different sounds and, as people experimented with the sounds, new instruments were created. Almost every culture has some form of drums, rattles, horns, flutes, and stringed instruments.

Rhythm sticks, rattles, shakers, bells, tambourines, and chimes, in addition to drums, do not require any special training to play. A simple rhythm can be played with any of these instruments, and several of them can be played together.

Prayer: Make a simple instrument out of found materials and play different rhythms. As you beat out the rhythm thank the Lord of the Dance for the wonderful gift of music in your life.

Singing

An old proverb says that he or she who sings prays twice. Having a beautiful voice is a gift but is not a necessity for prayer. Giving praise to the Lord through song is a multicultural tradition. From the Aborigines of Australia to the Native Americans of the United States, from the great music halls of Europe to the Incas of the Andes, the Lord's praises have been, and continue to be, sung.

Prayer: Choose a song, or write one of your own. Find a place where you feel comfortable, and raise your voice in song. Your song can express whatever emotions and feelings are inside of you. Let yourself feel your spirit rising on the wings of your song. It does not matter if your song is a mantra, the repetition of a single sound, a simple chant, or a complex piece of music. All song can be prayer if that is the intention in your heart.

Scripture and Music

Sometimes, a musical background can make a Scripture passage come alive to us. The music adds another dimension and enhances our understanding. While words often engage our thinking processes, music touches the heart.

Prayer: Choose a favorite Scripture passage, and find a piece of music that will enhance your reading of it. Instrumental pieces usually work well for this type of prayer. Read the words slowly as the music plays softly in the background, and allow the meaning of the passage to enter both your head and heart.

You might also try reading a longer story, such as the account of Creation, and choosing several musical selections to accompany it. Again, read the story slowly and let the words and music flow together to lead you to a deeper understanding.

"Music and religion are as intimately related as poetry and love."

—Will Durant

Scripture to Song

For those who are gifted with the musical-rhythmic intelligence, multiple or complex ideas can often be simplified by putting them to song. Most people are able to remember words sung in a song more easily than words read from a page.

Prayer: Select a passage from Scripture, and read it several times. Repeat the words until they have a rhythmic quality. Find one phrase that you can continually return to as the refrain. The song need not be original. You may use a tune you already know and write a paraphrase of the words in the Scripture. Sing aloud the passage, parable, or story you have put to song.

Tibetan Singing Bowls/Chimes

Creating ritual is important in both communal prayer and individual prayer. It is often helpful when entering into prayer to have a definite sign which signals the beginning. Tibetan Singing Bowls and chimes, frequently used in prayer in the Eastern traditions, are becoming very popular in the West due to their soft and melodic tones.

Prayer: Create a sacred space for prayer. It can be the corner of a room, an outdoor area, or any other place that invites you to reflection. Perhaps a candle will help to establish a prayerful environment. Sit in a position that is comfortable for you, and slowly tap the Tibetan singing bowl or chime. Let the tone reverberate. Feel it drawing you to a space deep within, and allow yourself to go there and listen in silence. You might choose to tap the bowl or chime again to indicate the end of your prayer time.

Music for Relaxation

Music has wonderfully healing properties. It can help us enter depths within ourselves not accessible by words. It quiets, calms, renews and refreshes. Music can lead us to solitude.

Prayer: Choose a piece of music that invites you to relax and enter into those deep, hidden spaces inside yourself. Do not try to think or put words to the music. Simply let it be music. Allow yourself to relax and be a part of the music. Flow with the rhythm and explore the new places that open up within you. Feel yourself as part of the rhythm of the universe.

> *"Music changes vibration and can restore balance.*
> *The heavy weight of our intellect can be balanced*
> *by the lighter spiritual energies absorbed through music."*
> —Stephanie Merritt

Musical Resources

Tape recorder
CD player
Headphones
Musical software
CDs and tapes
Keyboard
Homemade instruments
Multicultural instruments

Chapter four resources

Books

Bush, Carol A. *Healing Imagery and Music*. Rudra Press, 1995.

Doney, Meryl. *World Crafts: Musical Instruments*. Franklin Watts/Division of Grolier Publishing, 1995.

Gass, Robert with Kathleen Brehony. *Chanting: Discovering Spirit in Sound.* Broadway Books, 1999.

Hull, Arthur. *Drum Circle Spirit: Facilitating Human Potential through Rhythm.* White Cliffs Media, 1998.

Kavanaugh, Patrick. *The Spiritual Lives of Great Composers.* Zondervan, 1996.

Morgan, Marlo. *Message from Forever.* Cliff Street Books/Division of HarperCollins Publishers, 1998.

Merritt, Stephanie. *Mind, Music and Imagery*. Aslan, 1996.

Samuels, Michael, M.D. and Mary Rockwood Lane, R.N., M.S.N. *Creative Healing.* HarperCollins, 1998.

Electronic Sources

http://www.allonetribedrum.com/

http://www.benedictinesisters.org/vesp2.html

http://www.greatdreams.com/chanting.htm

Finding God through movement

CHAPTER FIVE

"Without the body the wisdom of the large self cannot be known."

—John Conger

Finding God through movement

The bodily-kinesthetic learners are gifted with coordination and dexterity and a powerful desire to be actively involved in whatever they are doing. One of the key pathways to the brain for these learners is through movement and through physical involvement. Traditional prayer forms with emphasis on silence and sitting do not adequately meet the prayer needs of these learners. These individuals understand intuitively the body-mind-spirit connection.

For these learners, effective prayer involves bodily movement of some kind. They need the opportunity to use their hands and feet and to feel the fluidity and grace of physical movement. Their God is one who knows how to dance and run and skip and jump. They are energized through movement and feel the Divine Source within them when they are active participants in prayer.

Eastern meditation techniques such as yoga and tai chi are especially helpful to the bodily-kinesthetic learners. They allow for movement while at the same time leading to calmness, tranquility, and a greater state of self-awareness. The very act of doing yoga or tai chi requires a great deal of concentration and focusing while actively engaging the body.

The use of manipulatives in prayer engages the bodily-kinesthetic learners. The opportunity to hold something in their hands, to light a candle, or to change positions from sitting to standing or kneeling will facilitate prayer for these individuals.

Using drama to reenact Gospel stories can also be a very prayerful experience for those blessed with the bodily-kinesthetic intelligence. Any type of drama will actively engage these learners and open new pathways to the Divine.

Sacred dance and liturgical movement are also invitations for the bodily-kinesthetic learner to explore new pathways to worship God. It is in and through physical involvement in prayer that they are transformed.

Sacred dance

"Why we dance: To dance is to pray, to pray is to heal, to heal is to give, to give is to live, to live is to dance."

—Native American

It is said that dance is the original form of sacred worship and can be found among the traditions of people the world over. From the Hawaiian hula to the drumbeats throughout the African continent, people use dance to worship. Our ancestors used dance since before recorded history, and dance continues to be a valuable tool for prayer that can be integrated with any spiritual path.

The Hawaiian hula signifies the intimate relationship between people and nature which was a fundamental part of early Hawaiian life. The gentle movements accompanied by chants reflect the early people's understanding of the sacredness of all of life and flow from a worldview in which "one's spirit might cycle through other living things after human death, or where beings with great mana (spiritual presence) might, at will, take on the form of other plants and animals around them. In such a worldview one could talk directly to the winds and rains and expect response, or swim with sharks, and being among beloved relatives, know you were completely safe in the ocean."

In her introduction to a video on African dance, Wyoma tells us that "the energy of African culture is primarily expressed by dancers…that native dancers have always used dance to express the deep African values of community, mutual respect, the importance of listening, and awareness of space. . ."

Dance also has a place in our own Biblical tradition. It was an integral part of the celebrations of ancient Israel, and numerous scriptural references refer to the use of dance in worship and celebration.

"Let Israel be glad in its Maker; the children of Zion rejoice in their King. Let them praise his name with dancing, making melody to him with tambourine and lyre."

—Psalm 149:2–3

"Praise him with tambourines and dance . . ."

—Psalm 150:4

"David danced before the lord with all his might . . ."

—2 Samuel 6:14

"Then the prophet Miriam, Aaron's sister, took a tambourine in her hand; and all the women went out after her with tambourines and with dancing."

—Exodus 15:20

To dance is to celebrate life with one's entire being. It can foster meditation and is an excellent alternative for those who have difficulty doing sitting meditation. It is a form of relaxation combining physical, mental, emotional, and spiritual energy. It draws its power and strength from both hemispheres of the brain since it requires both linear and non-linear involvement.

Dance is universal. The movements, gestures, and music have the potential of crossing linguistic, ethnic, and cultural barriers. To pray is to connect to the deepest level of our own beings as we seek God. Dance provides a vehicle to enhance this communication and connects us to these deeper realities. The engagement of the total body in prayer helps to remove distractions and enables us to focus clearly on what is essential.

Prayer: Select a piece of music, and allow your body to move to the rhythm; or select a story, event, or process to transform into a dance. Allow the Holy Spirit to move within you as you offer your entire being to God.

Multicultural music can enhance prayer by fostering cross-cultural connections. A comprehensive list of multicultural music selections is available in Chapter 4.

Discovery cards

"The mind's first step to self-awareness must be through the body."
—George Sheehan

There are innumerable activities each day which could open our minds and hearts to God, but we often don't take the time to do them because we are so busy and caught up in a whirlwind of "important" things to do. Discovery cards invite us to take the time to do something out of the ordinary, something that helps us to see the world differently, or something that allows God's presence to be seen in new and creative ways.

Think of all the beauty God puts before us each day that we never really see because we are too busy with the business of life. Discovery cards can enable us to say, "I want to be right here, right now, and take the time to see God's fingerprint in my own backyard."

Discovery cards may be written on index cards. Each card should contain a suggestion for something creative to do. Be inventive as you think of things to do that can open up new possibilities for discovering God in the midst of the ordinary.

The following are some suggestions, but creativity is built into this kind of prayer. Thousands of ideas are waiting to emerge.

Take a walk and look at a single flower. Examine the flower carefully. Notice its intricate design, its colors and shape. Thank God for the gift of flowers.

Smile at someone in the checkout line of a store today. Recall the Indian greeting Namaste, which means "May the God within me greet the God within you."

Hold a book in your hands. Think of all that happened to make that book a reality. Someone had a creative idea that he or she wanted to share. A teacher somewhere taught him or her the mechanics of writing to be able to capture the thought on paper Someone else facilitated the writing by designing the computer. Proofreaders, editors, and publishers all had hands in the final book you are holding. Don't forget to thank God for the tree that was used to provide the paper. Thank God for the gift of being able to read and write.

Take a one-minute break at work today. Just stop everything, and concentrate on breathing slowly in and out. Thank God for the gift of life.

Prayer: Choose a discovery card each morning. Read the card slowly, and consciously promise to do what the card suggests. You can discover God in new and surprising ways. In the midst of the ordinary, the extraordinary is ready to be uncovered.

A universal greeting

The Gandhi Foundation

I OFFER YOU PEACE
Face palms forward, elbows bent

I OFFER YOU FRIENDSHIP
Cup hands palm to palm, elbows bent

I OFFER YOU LOVE
Draw hands forward from heart

I HEAR YOUR NEEDS
Cup hands behind ears

I SEE YOUR BEAUTY
Cover eyes with hands and then uncover

I FEEL YOUR FEELINGS
Arms cross chest, fingertips to shoulders

MY WISDOM FLOWS FROM A HIGHER SOURCE
Move right hand, palm down, from head past face to meet upfacing left palm at chest, fingertips forward

I SALUTE THAT SOURCE IN YOU
Palms together in prayer position

LET US WORK TOGETHER
Fingers interlocked as two-handed fist

The prayer bag

"Whenever God intends to bring about any great thing,
he generally begins with a day of small things."
—George Whitefield

"Things" are everywhere around us. Sometimes there are so many things surrounding us that we don't really see any one thing at all. This prayer invites us to see one thing at a time and reflect on what it means. What wisdom is represented in a single object, whether natural or human-made? How has it come into our lives? What is its purpose? Who made it?

An alarm clock, a rock, a grain of rice, a pencil, a pipe cleaner, a computer disk, a small stuffed animal, a colorful cloth, a piece of ribbon, a notebook, a bottle of liquid paper ...the list can go on and on. Any item at all can be placed in the bag and used to remind us of the wisdom of God that surrounds us.

Prayer: Design a prayer bag by taking a brown paper bag and decorating it with paints, crayons, or any other media. You may also like to sew a cloth bag out of colorful fabric. When the bag is finished, choose a variety of objects from your environment that will fit into it.

Choose one item each day, and look at it with new eyes. Hold the item carefully, and examine it closely. What is the texture, the shape, the design? Is the surface smooth or rough? How do you use this item? What does it do to enrich your life or make your life easier? Thank God for the beauty of the item you are holding or for its utility. Pray for those who have enabled it to be in your hands.

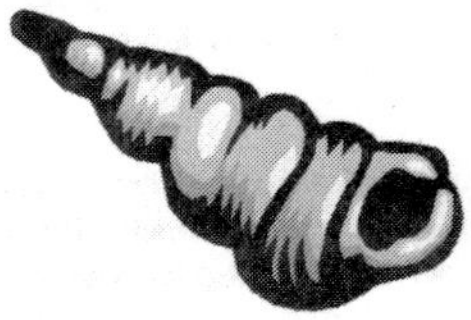

Prayer flags

Throughout the Himalayan countries, prayer flags can be seen everywhere—along pilgrimage routes, from the roofs of monasteries, in the mountain passes, from the eaves of homes, on tree branches, and on poles outside of public buildings. In the Tibetan language the word for prayer flag is lung ta, meaning "wind horse." When the wind blows, the prayer flags flap in the breeze and seem to carry the prayers of the believers to all the corners of the world.

In Buddhist tradition, prayer flags are reminders that each person is entrusted with the task of bringing goodness, virtue, healing, and happiness into the world; so, each time a Buddhist sees a prayer flag, it provides the opportunity for self-reflection. The colors of the Buddhist flags represent the five elements—blue for space, white for water, yellow for earth, green for air and wind, and red for fire. The pray-er inscribes quotes, prayers, and symbols to reflect his or her prayer for the world.

The ritual of creating a prayer flag, and hanging it outside to send one's prayers throughout the world, is applicable to any religious tradition. Quotes, prayers, colors, and symbols can be designed and added to reflect the deepest hopes and desires flowing out of one's own heart and into the heart of God filtered through one's own spiritual tradition.

Prayer: Select a piece of burlap or wide ribbon to create a prayer flag. You may wish to use natural found objects to weave twigs and/or grasses and flowers through the fabric, or use assorted paints and fabric markers to apply designs and write prayers or inspirational quotes on the banner. Attach the banner to a small branch or dowel, and tie a ribbon or piece of yarn for hanging.

When your prayer banner is completed, hang it from a tree or other outdoor object to allow your prayer to flow through the wind. At some point you may wish to display your prayer flag indoors.

Body movement as sacred

"Movement never lies. It is a barometer telling the state of the soul's weather to all who can read it."

—Martha Graham

Movement prayer invites us to connect at the deepest level with ourselves and all of humanity. This form of prayer leads us to become conscious of the God within our own bodies and to recognize the presence of God within others. Movement prayer allows us to let go of the need to use intellect and emotion and permits us to act and react from a more fundamental base. While Eastern prayer has always maintained a strong mind-body-spirit connection, we in the West are rediscovering this connection. Movement can be used with Psalms, scripture passages, poetry, songs, and stories. The possibilities are endless.

Prayer: Choose one of the following selections, and create movements to accompany the words. It might be helpful to record the passage on an audiocassette and perform the movements to the words.

Choose a psalm, such as the following:

Let me hear what God the Lord will speak,
for he will speak peace to his people,
to his faithful, to those who turn to him in their hearts.

Surely his salvation is at hand for those who fear him,
that his glory may dwell in our land.

Steadfast love and faithfulness will meet;
Righteousness and peace will kiss each other.
Faithfulness will spring up from the ground,
And righteousness will look down from the sky.

The Lord will give what is good,

and our land will yield its increase.
Righteousness will go before him,
And will make a path for his steps.

—Psalm 85:8–13

Choose a poem, such as the following:

The dark purple light rises in the north,
A yellow light rises in the east.
Then we of the flowers of the earth come forth
To receive a long life of joy.
We call ourselves the Butterfly Maidens.

Both male and female make their prayers to the east.
Make the respectful sign to the Sun our Creator.
The sounds of bells rings through the air,
Making a joyful sound throughout the land,
Their joyful echo resounding everywhere.

Humbly I ask my Father,
The perfect one, Taiowa, our Father,
The perfect one creating the beautiful life
Shown to us by the yellow light,
To give us perfect light at the time of the red light.

The perfect one laid out the perfect plan
And gave us a long span of life,
Creating song to implant joy in life.
On this path of happiness, we the Butterfly Maidens
Carry out his wishes by greeting our Father Sun.

The song resounds back from our Creator with joy,
And we of the earth repeat it to our Creator.

At the appearing of the yellow light,
Repeats and repeats again the joyful echo,
Sounds and resounds for times to come.[1]

or

Pieces

A world in pieces
A life in pieces . . .
We want to live new times, Lord God.
We want to see flourishing signs of hope
that we may put the pieces together.
and rebuild a united world.
We cry out for the Spirit of Unity,
so that from the four corners of the Earth
the breath of new life may caress all beings...
Come, Spirit of God,
spread over nations in conflict...
spread over groups and factions...
spread over gangs . . .
spread over . . .
May a new wind blow
to fill us with desire and strength
so the pieces may become one body
the world's body
the people's body
because you created us as one,
and that is how you want us to be.[2]

—Ernesto Barros Cardoso, Brazil

[1]Waters, Frank. *Book of Hopi*. Ballantine Books, 1971. p. 7.

[2]Tirabassi, Maren C. and Kathy Wonson Eddy. *Gifts of Many Cultures*. Clevland:United Church Press, 1995.

Choose a prayer:

Our Father who art in heaven,
hallowed be thy name.
Thy Kingdom come, thy will be done,
On earth as it is in heaven.

Give us this day our daily bread
and forgive us our trespasses
as we forgive those who trespass against us.

Lead us not into temptation,
but deliver us from evil.
(For thine is the Kingdom and the power
and the glory now and forever). Amen.

or

Lord, teach me to be generous.
Teach me to serve you as you deserve;
to give and not to count the cost;
to fight and not to heed the wounds;
to toil and not to seek for rest;
to labor and not to ask for reward,
except to know
that I am doing your will.

—Prayer of St. Ignatius of Loyola

Choose one of the following scripture passages:

Come, you that are blessed by my Father, inherit the kingdom prepared for you from the foundation of the world; for I was hungry and you gave me food, I was thirsty and you gave me something to drink, I was a stranger and you welcomed me, I was naked and you gave me clothing, I was sick and you took care of me, I was in prison and you visited me . . . .

—Matthew 25:34–37

There will be signs in the sun, the moon and the stars, and on the earth distress among nations confused by the roaring of the sea and the waves . . . Now when these things begin to take place, stand up and raise your heads, because your redemption is drawing near.

—Luke 21:25, 28

The spirit of the Lord is upon me, because he has anointed me to bring good news to the poor. He has sent me to proclaim release to the captives and recovery of sight to the blind, to let the oppressed go free, to proclaim the year of the Lord's favor.

—Luke 4:18–19

Choose a song:

Many songs will lend themselves to interpretative movement. The following are some of the artists or groups whose songs are among my favorites. Choose one of their songs or a favorite of your own and create sacred actions that convey the words of the song.

The Dameans
Ducote, Darryl
Dufford, SJ, Bob
Haas, David
Haugen, Marty
Joncas, Michael
Peña, Donna
Schutte, Dan
Sherman, Kathy
The Taizé Community
Walker, Christopher

These psalms, prayers, poems, scripture passages, and songs are only suggestions. As you feel more comfortable with body movement as prayer, you will find selections of your own that can be interpreted in this free-flowing form of prayer that connects the body, mind, and spirit.

The field-trip prayer

"If you begin to live life looking for the God that is all around you every moment becomes a prayer."

—Frank Bianco

We know that God is all around us. It might have been much easier, however, for our ancestors to see God in the beauty of creation which surrounded them than it is for modern people in our concrete-and-glass world. Indeed God is equally as present in our lives today, but it we need to train ourselves to slow down and make a conscious effort to see him in the world.

The intricate design of a leaf, the myriad shades of colors in ponds and lakes, the majesty of mountains, and the simplicity of clouds all call us to prayer in a natural way. However, our lives and days are often filled with office meetings, trips to the grocery store, visits to the doctor's office, sitting in a classroom, and having lunch at a favorite restaurant. These, too, can call us to prayer if we open ourselves to God in new ways.

Buddhists tell of "becoming aware," which is often taught through breathing techniques and concentration. There is another kind of awareness readily available to all Christians. It is the awareness of the present moment and of God's presence in that moment. God is always present in all the moments of our lives, but it is we, however, who are often not aware of him.

The field-trip prayer invites us to choose one activity in our daily schedule and approach it much like a school field trip—with anticipation and a sense of excitement about what we might discover or learn.

A Trip to the Grocery Store (with Awareness)

I get in the car and turn the key. What a marvel of ingenuity that the car starts! I thank God for all those whose gifts of creativity and genius made the car a reality. I drive into the parking lot of the local grocery store, and there is no space to park near the door. However, instead of becoming impatient, I thank God that I am healthy enough to walk to the door.

I enter the store and am just on the verge of becoming totally discouraged at the crowds, when I stop myself and reflect on the incredible diversity in humanity. I notice the children with their moms and dads, the teenagers at the checkout counter, the clerks restocking the shelves, and the elderly with their canes and walkers maneuvering down the aisles.

As I begin filling my basket, I remind myself of what a gift it is to have food readily available. I pray for God to supply the needs of those who don't. I go to the produce department and pick up a few tomatoes. I remember the migrant farm workers whose sweat and toil have brought these tomatoes to the market. The bananas I pick up call me to think of the struggles of those in Central America whose wages are often not enough to live on, and I pray for them and ask God to help me know what I can do to help.

I put paper products in my basket and think of all it took to bring these products to me. I am grateful for the choices available to me, but also think of those who have no choices. I stop for just a moment and reflect on how many paper products I use and the cost in trees. Could I make better choices? Could I learn to live with less? What is God's voice telling me?

There are so many cookies and cakes to choose from, but because I am shopping with awareness I stop before adding them to the basket and ask myself, "How will this be of nutritional value to me?" "How will this product help me to show respect and care of my body, God's temple?" I decide that one small bag of cookies is enough. I really don't need that German chocolate cake!

There are aisles and aisles filled with canned goods, but I think about what I need and remind myself that there is a difference between needs and wants. I ask God to help me choose more consciously only what I need.

Every aisle becomes an opportunity for prayer as I make conscious choices instead of just throwing things in the basket. I notice the people around me and take the time to smile. I offer assistance to the old man who cannot reach the top shelf.

I shop with awareness.

This type of prayer is not easy because it means having to reflect on why we do what we do. It is so much easier to just do things without thinking about them. But, then, we miss seeing God in the events of our lives.

Prayer: Look at your calendar of events for the week. Choose just one activity you will do with awareness. Perhaps it is a trip to the doctor's office or a boring task at your job. Ask God to help you live with awareness and lead you to transformation through the everyday routines of your life.

Once you begin to pray this way, you will discover that God seems to "pop up" in the most unexpected places—and it will be because you have eyes to see, ears to hear, and a heart that is open.

Ten shin go so

"Listen to what you know through your body."
—Taisen Deshimaru

Ten shin go so is an exercise developed by tai chi and aikido masters to facilitate both physical and mental focus. It combines physical movement with a storyline to energize the body, to calm oneself, and to direct mental attention.[1]

Prayer: The following is a suggested exercise. Try it a few times until you are comfortable with the movements and they flow naturally.

Begin by standing with feet shoulder-width apart.
Relax hands at your side.
Storyline: You place yourself in a position of openness.

Inhale to the count of eight
Hold your breath to the count of eight.
Exhale to the count of eight. (3 times)
Storyline: You calm yourself inwardly and outwardly.

Inhale. Raise hands in a wide arc above head.
Palms open and extended outward.
Storyline: You invite the energy of the universe into your being.

Exhale. Bring hands downward and cross over heart.
Storyline: You acknowledge God within.

Inhale. Open hands outward with palms extended towards the earth.
Storyline: You offer the goodness and wisdom within you to the world.

Exhale and return to starting position.
Inhale to the count of eight.
Hold your breath to the count of eight
Exhale to the count of eight. (3 times)
Storyline: You rest in the silence.

Design a ten shin go so exercise of your own. Simply put together movement with ideas for a storyline that is prayerful for you.

---

[1]Campbell, Linda, Bruce Campbell and Dee Dickinson. *Teaching and Learning Through Multiple Intelligences.* Allyn & Bacon, 1999.

Yoga

Yoga fosters the integration of body, mind, and spirit. It was developed in India thousands of years ago, but because it deals with universal truths, its practice is as relevant today as it was then. Yoga is not a religion in itself but an aid to self-awareness and relaxation. It is applicable to any religious tradition. The philosophy of yoga sees the body as a vehicle for the soul's journey toward wholeness, toward enlightenment through awareness.

Yoga includes a system of exercising to increase self-discipline based on the tenets of "simple living and high thinking."[1] The exercise, however, is more than just body movement. The asanas (a Sanskrit word meaning "steady pose") combine relaxed movement, deep breathing, and mental concentration. The practice of yoga can enhance one's prayer life by opening up new pathways to the God.

Prayer: Find a quiet place each morning, and begin your prayer with some simple yoga exercises. As your body stretches and relaxes with the different poses, allow your mind to open itself to God's voice.

[1] Sivananda Yoga Vedanta Center. *Yoga Mind and Body*. DK Publishing, 1998.

A potpourri of bodily-kinesthetic ideas for prayer

"The physical language of the body is so much more powerful than words."
—Bill Irwin

Praying with your Camera

The world is filled with the handiwork of God. The following prayer by Rabbi Joshua Abraham Heschel might well be called the photographer's prayer:

> *Dear Lord, grant me the grace of wonder. Surprise me,*
> *amaze me, awe me in every crevice of your universe . . .*
> *Each day enrapture me with your marvelous things*
> *without number. I do not ask to see the reason for it*
> *all. I ask only to share the wonder of it all.*

Prayer: Take your camera, and go for a leisurely walk. Use all of your senses to open yourself to the world around you. Listen for God's voice speaking to you in your surroundings, and capture the details on film. You may choose to simply pray with the pictures at a later date or use them as a stimulus for a journal entry.

The Puzzle Prayer

The very act of putting a puzzle together can be very relaxing. A puzzle with a beautiful scene can invite us to seem to enter into the scene and place ourselves in the midst of flowers, on a mountaintop, or at the ocean's shore.

Prayer: Choose a jigsaw puzzle with the number of pieces with which you feel comfortable. Find a quiet place where you can work on the puzzle undisturbed over a period of time. Begin your puzzle session with a prayer for clarity—that you may know how the pieces of your life fit together. Be open and attentive to the silence and to the word of God present in the silence.

Pray with Clay

The Bible reminds us of how we are like clay in the hands of the Master Potter. Praying with clay invites us to enter into the creative act much as God the Creator does—by feeling the consistency, molding the creation, perhaps destroying it, and molding it again.

Prayer: Take some clay, and squish it through your fingers. Play with it. Have fun with it. Form balls and snake shapes. Become comfortable with it. Then create a form with it. Place your newly formed piece in a special place, and let it remind you that you are as clay in God's hands.

Tai Chi

Tai chi is a moving form of yoga and meditation combined. In Chinese philosophy the word chi symbolizes the vital force that animates the body. The goal of the practice of tai chi is to foster the circulation of the chi within the body. Another primary aim of tai chi is to lead the practitioner to a calm and tranquil state through the precise execution of the exercises. This tranquility opens us in unique ways to hear God's voice in our lives.

Prayer: Learn some of the basic tai chi moves, and incorporate them into your daily prayer. Allow the movements to flow freely as you focus your attention on executing them with precision and grace. The movements themselves will lead you to a prayerful state. Thank God for the grace and fluidity of your body.

Windsock Prayer

Windsocks are very pleasing to the eye as they wave in the breeze. The bright colors and fluid motion of a windsock can symbolize our willingness to be carried on the wings of God's love.

Prayer: Make a windsock by using construction paper and crepe paper. Decorate a sheet of construction paper with a bright design. Roll the finished drawing into a cylinder, and staple it. Take 4 to 6 sheets of crepe paper approximately 3 feet in length. Write prayers of petition and thanksgiving on the crepe paper. Staple the strips to the construction paper. Attach a piece of string to the top of the construction paper, and fly your windsock outdoors. Feel your prayers winging their way to God as the breezes move your windsock throughout the day.

Chapter five resources

Books

Ansari, Mark and Liz Lark. *Yoga for Beginners.* Perennial, 1999.

Austin, Miriam. *Yoga for Wimps: Poses for the Flexibly Impaired.* Sterling, 1999.

Campbell, Linda, Bruce Campbell and Dee Dickinson. *Teaching and Learning Through Multiple Intelligences.* Allyn & Bacon, 1998.

Chu, Vincent. *Beginner's Tai Chi Chuan.* Unique Publications, 2000.

Chuen, Lam Kam. *Step-By-Step Tai Chi.* Fireside Publishers, 1994.

Dang, Tri Thong. *Beginning T'ai Chi.* Charles E. Tuttle, 1994.

Dorr, Donal. *Integral Spirituality.* Orbis Books, 1990.

Khalsa, Shakta. *Fly Like A Butterfly: Yoga for Children.* Sterling, 1999.

Knaster, Mirka. *Discovering the Body's Wisdom.* Bantam Books, 1998.

Miller, Elise Browning and Carol Blackman. *Life Is a Stretch: Easy Yoga, Anytime, Anywhere.* Llewellyn, 1999.

Roth, Gabrielle. *Sweat Your Prayers: Movement as Spiritual Practice.* J. P. Tarcher/Putnam, 1998.

Sivananda Yoga Vedanta Center. *Yoga Mind and Body*. DK, 1998.

Tirabassi, Maren C. and Kathy Wonson Eddy. *Gifts of Many Cultures.* Pilgrim Press, 1995

Waters, Frank. *Book of the Hopi.* Ballantine Books, 1971.

Wilkens, Deirdré Korff. *Multiple Intelligences Activities.* Teacher Created Materials, 1996.

Yee, Rodney. *Yoga: The Poetry of the Body*. St. Martin's, 2002.

Zhang, Fuxing. *Handbook of T'ai Chi Ch'uan Exercises.* Red Wheel/Weiser, 1996.

Videos

African Healing Dance. *Wyoma and the Dancers and Drummers of DAMBALLA.* Sounds True, 1997.

A.M./P.M. Yoga for Beginners. Rodney Yee and Patricia Walden. VHS. Living Arts, 1998.

Tai Chi—6 Forms, 6 Easy Lessons. DVD. Paul Lam. Wellspring Media, 1998.

Tai Chi for Busy People. DVD. Dr. Keith Jeffery. Terra Entertainment, 2000.

T'ai Chi Ch'uan. VHS. Ken Kersh. Victory Multimedia, 1994.

Yoga Journal's Yoga for Meditation. Rodney Yee. VHS. Living Arts, 1996.

Electronic Sources

http://www.prayerflags.com (prayer flags)

http://www.fourgates.com/flags.asp (prayer flags)

http:www.mgf-hawaii.com/hula.htm (hula)

http://wholeliferesources.com/sacred_dance.htm (sacred dance)

Finding God through nature

CHAPTER SIX

"Look deep into nature, and then you will understand everything better."

—Albert Einstein

Finding God through nature

This is the most recent intelligence identified by Gardner, yet it is probably one of the earliest recognized by Native and Aboriginal peoples throughout the world. The capacity to live in harmony with nature has long been a hallmark of Native Americans and other indigenous peoples on every continent.

A very personal experience several years ago helped me to understand just how deeply some native people feel connected to nature and how distant we in the Western world have become. I was working in the rainforest of northeastern Guatemala. Early one morning, as I was waking up, I heard voices on the river. I was sleeping in a thatched-roof hut and had a clear view of the river from the open space between the roof and the low wall. I saw several of the Maya in their small dugout cayucos (canoes) throwing tortillas into the water. My first thought was "How can they be throwing that food in the water when we don't even have enough to eat ourselves?" However, before making a judgment I went to find one of my Maya friends to ask what they were doing. His response: "Today the people are going to fish, and one never takes something from nature without giving something back." Hence, they were offering tortillas to the river and to the creatures that inhabited the river.

I have thought and prayed often about what I learned that day. What if we all believed as the Maya do—that one never takes something from nature without giving something back? How different our world would be.

The Maya I have known certainly exhibit the naturalist intelligence. They are gifted with the ability to identify and use the natural flora and fauna in their environment. They see the interconnectedness of all living things; the plants and animals hold an important place in the scheme of life which we, too, are part of. They have a natural reverence for all of creation and a deep understanding that the Creator is at the center of all of life.

The Naturalist form of prayer invites us to see ourselves as part of the great cosmic story; it invites us to stand still and look at the world around us and to reflect on our role in it. Patterns in nature suggest a master plan; taking the time to situate oneself in nature can lead to deep contemplation.

What speaks to me of God?

"Every time you admire something in nature, it's a prayer to the Creator."

—Vernon Harper

The beauty of the trees,
the softness of the air,
the fragrance of the grass,
speaks to me.

The summit of the mountain,
the thunder of the sky,
the rhythm of the sea,
speaks to me.

The faintness of the stars,
the freshness of the morning,
the dewdrop on the flower,
speaks to me . . .

—Chief Dan George

Prayer: How does nature speak to you of God? Look around you, and write as many verses as you choose following the pattern.

____

____

____
speaks to me of God.

____

____

____
speaks to me of God.

____

____

____
speaks to me of God.

Nature observation prayer

Every day, mysteries unfold right before our eyes, but we do not see them. We are busy. We have so much to do. We have so many commitments. We live life running from one activity to another looking for happiness, and kick aside the rocks in our path that seem to prevent us from obtaining it. Rarely do we look down and realize that the very road we are on at any single given moment in time is a gift from God.

Observation of nature provides us with the opportunity to stop for a few moments to see what is happening right before our eyes. It invites us to sit still and see the mysteries of the visible world—beauty, growth, change, death, new life—and, in clearly seeing the visible world, to come to know that which we cannot see.

Prayer: Find a spot outdoors or near a window where you can observe nature and sit undisturbed for at least 15 minutes. Do nothing but look at what is happening in that spot.

Notice the colors, not just green or yellow,
red or orange,
but how many shades of green?
How many shades of yellow?
How many shades of red or orange?

Thank God . . .
for the beauty of color in your life,
for the vibrant reds, and yellows and blues,
for the softer lavenders, turquoise and mint greens,
for the earth tones, the browns and beiges, golds and grays.

Think about the colors in your life at this moment in time.
What are they? How can you express your
gratitude to God the Master Artist for the colors
of your life?

How many shapes do you see?
Round, triangular, square,
hexagonal, trapezoidal, oval?

Thank God . . .
for the geometry of things in your own life,
for the shapes and forms that make up the patterns
along your life's journey.

What shapes describe your life right now?

What kinds of trees do you see? Choose one, and
look at it carefully.
What does the trunk look like?
How large is it? Can your arms reach around it?
Can you feel the texture? Is it rough or smooth?
How are the branches formed?

Are there leaves on the tree? What types of leaves?
What shapes are they? What colors are they?
Why are these trees growing in this environment?
What supports and nourishes them?

Thank God . . .
for the support and nourishment he constantly
gives to you in your environment.
What or who is the source of support
and nourishment in your life?

Is fertilizer needed to make your environment
more conducive to growth?

What do you need to add to the soil of your life
to make it more productive?

Are there flowers blooming in your spot?
What colors are they? How are the petals formed?
What insects are attracted to them?

If the flowers are not blooming,
think about the seeds or bulbs in the ground.
What will they become when they emerge from the dark, moist soil?

Thank God . . .
for the beauty of the flowers and the beauty in your own life.
What or who are the things or persons of beauty in your life?
How do you thank them for the joy they have given you?

If you do not see the flowers, thank God for the seeds and bulbs
which will emerge in the spring.
Think about the seeds of possibility lying dormant within you.
What is God calling you to be?
How is God calling you to bring beauty into the world?

Are you receiving the moisture and sunshine necessary to bloom?

If not, what do you need to do?

Notice an insect in your spot.

It might be a brilliantly colored butterfly or a tiny ant.

What does the insect look like?

How is it shaped?

What distinguishes it from other insects?

What can it do?

What is its food source?

What does it bring to its environment?

How is it suited to its environment?

Thank God . . .

for the little things in life you take for granted, and ask for the gift of knowing your place in the world as does the ant or the butterfly.

What distinguishes you from others?

How does the work you do resonate with your inner being?

Is there harmony and balance in your life?

What else are you observing in your spot?

Choose one thing, and reflect upon it by asking yourself questions about it.

Then, thank God for the gifts revealed to you through your reflections.

I am looking at a(n) ____________________________.

My thoughts:

My prayer:

The tree prayer

"A tree uses what comes its way to nurture itself. By sinking its roots deeply into the earth, by accepting the rain that flows towards it, by reaching out to the sun, the tree perfects its character and becomes great . . . Absorb, absorb, absorb. That is the secret of the tree."

—Deng Ming-Dao

In her book titled *Point of Power: A Relationship with Your Soul*, author Kay Snow-Davis uses the image of a tree to symbolize what she sees as four natural rhythms within people: root, trunk, branch, and leaf. She explains that an individual's point of power is the unique combination of root, trunk, branch, and leaf within each of us and that an understanding of one's own and others natural rhythms can lead to greater self-acceptance and acceptance of others.[1]

Here is a summary of Snow-Davis' ideas:

The Root is the Sustainer. Your senses allow you to absorb life's experiences as the roots of a tree absorb water. With great ease you can do one thing for a long period of time and you would prefer to not be disturbed. New sounds, sights, and textures interest you. As you are working on things new ideas develop, rarely in an ordered fashion.

The Trunk is the Maintainer. You are in place to keep systems in order. You are very reliable and solid in friendships and other relationships. Consistency is your friend and you are not fond of interruptions. Change is not a bad thing for you, provided you are given some warning beforehand. Objects and information that can be manipulated with your hands are much easier for you to work with.

The Branch is the Translator and helps bring ideas into order. You are particularly fond of the beginning stages of any project: the brainstorming, creating, experimenting, and discussion. To be interrupted from your task is not a big deal and any suggestions you may receive when interrupted are alright provided you may use them at your discretion. You may be less likely to see a project to its end because you are looking for a new and exciting project to begin with anew.

The Leaf is the Visionary. It is rare to find your mind at rest, you are instead always in motion. New ideas form within your mind and just as quickly you move on to the next project. Each idea is instantly done when it is in your mind, even if it is not fully formed. Frustration may occur when you have to describe your ideas to people who are different from you. You are very capable of juggling all of life's tasks at one time.

Prayer: Meditate on a tree. What are your greatest strengths? What is your natural rhythm—that of the root, trunk, branch, or leaf? Remember, you are a combination of all the elements of a tree, but some elements are more dominant than others.

Are you primarily a root person who engages all of your senses in the daily experience of life? Do you acquire knowledge through a hands-on interaction with your environment? Do you work better in quiet surroundings without disturbances?

Are you primarily a trunk person, whose strength maintains order and tranquility in an environment? Are you a detail person, one who can take multiple pieces and put them all together into a coherent whole?

Are you primarily a branch person whose mind grasps multiple concepts simultaneously? Are you an enthusiastic beginner of projects but one whose interest wanes when the initial creative energy is exhausted and it is time to attend to the details? Are you able to present your ideas in such a way that the root and trunk can help bring them to fruition?

Are you primarily a leaf person whose mind is in constant motion dreaming and creating? Does your mind move faster than your body can respond? Do you have difficulty explaining your ideas to others? Do you find yourself engaged in many tasks at the same time?

Pray for the gift of self-knowledge. Thank God for the wonderfully unique combination of traits that you are. Celebrate your giftedness and pray that you might be patient and understanding when living and working with others whose gifts differ from yours.

---

[1] Snow-Davis, Kay. *Point of Power: A Relationship with Your Soul*. Harper Collins, 1995.

Psalms of praise to the creator

"The universe is but one vast symbol of God."
—Thomas Carlyle

The psalms provide a wonderful model for litanies or hymns of praise for the magnificent gifts of creation. By using the models provided by a number of the psalms, we can create our own hymns of praise.

Prayer: Choose one or more of the patterns below, and compose your own psalm of praise in thanksgiving for creation.

O Lord, our Sovereign,
how majestic is your name in
all the earth!
—Psalm 8:1

Fill in the lines (add more if you need to!) with the gifts of creation that inspire you to echo the words of the psalmist.

____

____

____

____

____

____

O Lord, our Sovereign,
how majestic is your name in
all the earth!

We give thanks to you, O God;
We give thanks; your name is near.

—from Psalm 75:1

For the marvel of ____________________,

We give thanks to you, God.

For the marvel of ____________________,

We give thanks to you, God.

For the marvel of ____________________,

We give thanks to you, God.

Bless the Lord, O my soul
O Lord my God, you are very great.
You are clothed with honor and majesty,
Wrapped in light as with a garment.
You stretch out the heavens like a tent,
You set the beams of your chambers on the waters,
You make the clouds your chariot,
You ride on the wings of the wind,
You make the winds your messengers,
Fire and flame your ministers.

—from Psalm 104:1–4

Recount the wonders of creation in your own words.

You ________________________________

You ________________________________

You ________________________________

You ________________________________

O give thanks to the Lord, for he is good;
For his steadfast love endures forever.

—from Psalm 107:1

Give thanks to the Lord for
____________________;
his love endures forever.

Give thanks to the Lord, for
____________________;
his love endures forever.

Give thanks to the Lord, for
____________________;
his love endures forever.

I will extol you, my God and King,
And bless your name forever and ever.

—from Psalm 145

I will bless your name for ____________________.

I will bless your name for ____________________.

I will bless your name for ____________________.

I will bless your name forever and ever.

Praise him, sun and moon;
Praise him, all you shining stars!
Praise him, you highest heavens,
And you waters above the heavens!

—from Psalm 148:3–4

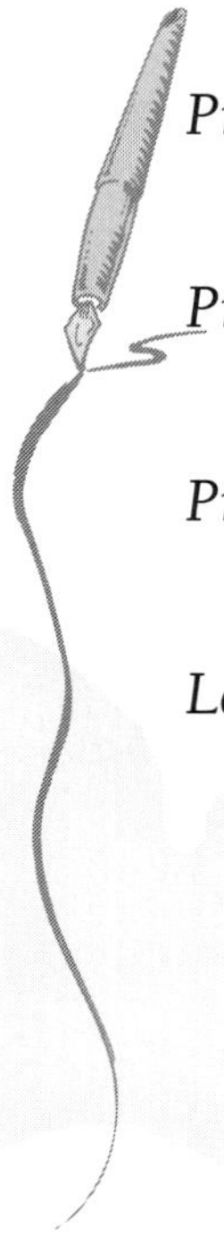

Praise him, ________________,

Praise him, ________________,

Praise him, ________________.

Let them all praise the name of the Lord

A prayer stick

"Making prayer sticks is a way to access what is already there, though sometimes mysteriously hidden from our immediate awareness."

—Nancy Wells

The making of prayer sticks is a tradition among many Native American peoples of the United States and Canada. The purpose of the prayer stick is to help focus energy on those aspects of one's life that need healing. There is no one specific way to make a prayer stick. The essential component is a stick, usually one that is forked, though this is not essential. Different colored yarns and ribbons, feathers, and other natural objects can be attached to the prayer stick. The movement of feathers, according to some Native American tribes, signifies one's prayer rising to the heavens. Each object placed on the stick should symbolize something important to the maker. According to Nancy Wells,

> *"Every color of yarn, every object attached to the prayer stick contains the energy of the prayer. Making prayer sticks is a way of asking the Great Spirit to help us stay in touch with our essential being so that we can blossom and radiate as naturally and as wildly as the dandelion. As the seed contains the tree, so do each of us contain all of our infinite possibilities."*[1]

Prayer: Take a walk to enjoy the sights and sounds of your environment. As you walk, look for a branch from a tree that can be the base of your prayer stick. Sit with the branch quietly, and thank God for the life this branch represents. Paint the stick, or wrap some yarn or ribbon pieces around it. Find a feather or two and other natural objects, and attach them as well. Think about the objects you are placing on your prayer stick and what each has to teach you. Offer a prayer to God in thanksgiving for the gifts of nature and your desire to open your heart to the message each gift contains.

Place your prayer stick outdoors in the ground, if possible.

---

[1]Wells, Nancy. *Return to Earth: Spirit and Memory.* Online posting. March 2, 2002. http://www.ncf.org/exhibits/return/exh_return_wells.html

Did you hear? Did you see?

"If you wish to know the divine, feel the wind on your face and the warm sun on your hand."
—The Buddha

In her book titled *Did You Hear Wind Sing Your Name?*[1], Sandra De Coteau Orie, an Oneida Indian writer, artisan, and educator, recounts her people's song of spring.

Traveling North
Did you see
Spirit Hawk dancing on the Wind?

Did you feel
morning Sun's warmth upon your face
welcoming you to a new day?

Did you smell
the sweet scent of the sacred Cedar?

Did you hear
Wind sing your name?
Does your memory bring Sweet Grass's fragrance?

Did you taste
the Thunderer's moist sky Waters?
Were you healed by Meadow's wild Strawberries?...

Prayer: Adapting Ms. De Coteau Orie's pattern, use your senses to appreciate the nature around you. Take a walk, sit in a scenic spot, or look out of your window, and experience nature through all of your senses during different seasons of the year. Give thanks to the Creator who has so gifted you with such wonders all around you.

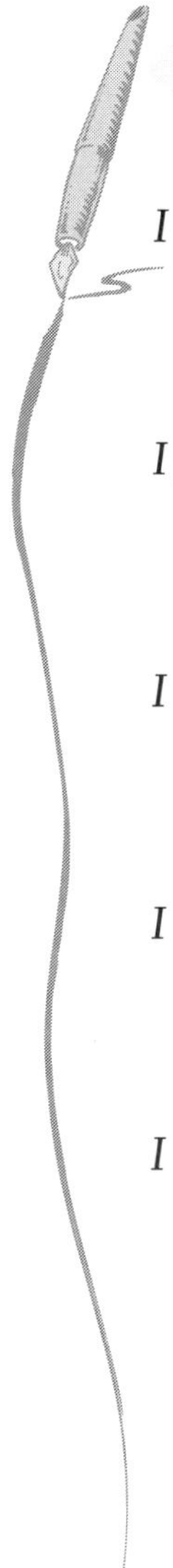

*I see*____

*I feel*____

*I smell*____

*I hear*____

*I taste*____

---

[1]De Coteau Orie, Sandra. *Did You Hear the Wing Sing Your Name?*. Walker, 1996.

Flower petal prayer

"Flowers are beautiful hieroglyphics of nature, with which she indicates how much she loves us."

—Wolfgang von Goethe

The reds, greens, yellows, blues, purples, magentas, and myriad other colors of flowers remind us of the artistry of God the Creator. Delicate blossoms unfurling in the early morning dew, blossoms that close with the evening sunset, the annuals, and the perennials all teach us something of God the Divine Artist. It is the very variety of flowers in a garden that gives it great beauty. The flower petal prayer invites us to thank God for the beauty in our own lives. Petal by petal we look at that which gives us joy and that which is in God's hands alone. The flower petal prayer grows daily over the course of a week as we add a new petal each day of those things in our lives for which we are grateful or the situations/events in our lives which we bring before the Lord to ask for guidance and help.

Prayer: Cut seven petals out of colored paper. Put them in a special place. Each day at prayer, choose one petal and hold it in your hand. Be still, and allow all that is within you to surface in the silence. After a period of reflection, write on the petal something you are grateful for or something you would like guidance about. Glue the petal around a circle on a contrasting sheet of colorful paper. At the end of the week, your prayer flower will be complete. It represents things which you hope for and dream about and things for which you come before God with gratitude and thanksgiving.

A potpourri of nature ideas for prayer

A Photo-Language Prayer

We cannot always find ourselves praying in a forest, near a stream, in the mountains, or next to the ocean. Oftentimes, we are surrounded by concrete, glass, skyscrapers, and apartment buildings. For times when we wish to pray in the presence of God's handiwork but cannot, we can use photos of nature scenes as visual substitutes.

Prayer: Choose a photo of a nature scene from a magazine or from your own collection. Imagine yourself in the scene. Perhaps it is sitting by the side of a mountain stream or walking through the rainforest. Allow yourself to imagine what the place sounds like and smells like. Listen to what the place has to teach you about God. How is God present to you in the stream? Along the path? Feel yourself an integral part of God's Creation; feel your interconnectedness with all that surrounds you. Give praise and thanksgiving to the One who has so blessed your life and continually fills it with beauty and meaning.

"Nature is an unlimited broadcasting station through which
God speaks to us every hour, if we only will tune in."

—George Washington Carver

Nature's Recordings

There are many nature recordings available today. Recordings of ocean waves, mountain streams, rainforests, and thunderstorms can lead us to a place inside ourselves where we become a part of the great cosmic story. We can enter into new environments through sound.

Prayer: Choose an audio recording of sounds of nature. Close your eyes and allow yourself to enter into the scene it evokes. Feel yourself in the ocean with the waves washing over you or lying under a palm tree listening to the sounds of the dolphins. Enter into the sound, and hear God's voice inviting you to be a part of this magnificent act of creation. Give thanks and praise for the invitation to be a part of something much greater than yourself.

Nature's Treasure Hunt

We are surrounded by evidence of God the Master Artist, yet oftentimes we fail to see what is right in front of us. Prayer can call us to look around to see things that can be seen only when we are not hidden by the veil of busyness.

Prayer: Take a walk around your neighborhood, and—paraphrasing the words of T. S. Elliott—see that place for the first time. Pick up a leaf or stone, a pebble or seashell, an acorn or blade of grass. Place in a small bag the items you find. When you are finished collecting, choose a place to sit quietly and pray with the items. Take each one by itself, and study its uniqueness. Allow yourself to be amazed by the veins on the leaf or the blend of colors on the blade of grass. Recall the Scripture passage in which Jesus talks of the Father's concern for the birds of the air and the flowers of the field (Luke 12:22–32). Give thanks for the simple things of life, for the blade of grass, the pebbles underfoot, the flowers blooming—and resolve to walk through life noticing more of the grandeur of God which surrounds you.

The Seed Prayer

Jesus was fond of using natural objects to lead people to prayer. In the parable of the sower (Luke 8:4–8, 11–15), the seed is a metaphor for the word of God. We understand that if seeds fall on rock or is trampled underfoot and carried off by birds, it cannot grow as the farmer intended. Jesus used this image of the seed to help us understand the importance of cultivating within ourselves and in others good "soil" in which the word of God can flourish.

Prayer: Take an ordinary seed, perhaps a flower seed, and hold it in your hand. It has the potential to become something beautiful, but it will never reach its potential if it remains in your hand. It must be placed in the darkness of the soil and have the right conditions and care to develop into a thing of beauty. As you hold the seed, reflect on your Christian life. What potential your life has to show forth the beauty of the Gospel! Are you cultivating the soil of your heart for the seed of the word? How are you nurturing the seed? Are you taking the time to water it and fertilize it occasionally?

Now plant the seed in a container. Push it gently into the soil, and give it some water. Watch it as it emerges from the soil and reaches toward the sun. And pray that, like the seed, God's word in you will grow to maturity. As you water and fertilize your seed, take time to ask yourself how you are nourishing and watering your soul. Give food and water to your soul today.

i thank you god for this most amazing day:
For the leaping greenly spirits of trees and a
Blue true dream of sky; and for everything
Which is natural which is infinite which is yes

—E. E. Cummings

Chapter six resources

Books

Berry, Thomas. *The Great Work*. Harmony/Bell Tower, 2000.

De Coteau Orie, Sandra. *Did You Hear the Wind Sing Your Name?* Walker, 1996.

Elgin, Duane. *Promise Ahead*. HarperCollins, 2000.

Hartmann, Thom. *The Last Hours of Ancient Sunlight*. Harmony Books, 1999.

Jones, Shirley (editor). *Simply Living*. New World Library, 1999.

Jung, Shannon. *We Are Home: A Spirituality of the Environment*. Paulist Press, 1993.

Macy, Joanna and Molly Brown. *Coming Back to Life: Practices to Reconnect Our Lives, Our World*. New Society Publishers, 1998.

Medicine Eagle, Brooke. *The Last Ghost Dance*. Ballantine, 2000.

Sams, Jamie. *Earth Medicine*. HarperCollins, 1994.

Snow-Davis, Kay. *Point of Power: A Relationship with Your Soul*. HarperCollins, 1995.

Electronic Sources

Andrews, Ted. *"Magical Prayer Sticks."* Online posting. http://kittyshaman.tripod.com/prayerstick.html

Wesling, Nanci. *"Tools for Transformation: Discover Your Point of Power."* Online posting. http://www.featherhawk.com/articles

Nature Sounds

Mountain Streams: Nature's Relaxing Sounds. CD. Masters Intercontinental, 1997.

Nature's Relaxing Sounds: Tropical Rain Forest. CD. Masters Intercontinental, 1997.

Rain Storms: Sounds of Nature. CD. Masters Intercontinental, 1997.

Sounds of the Earth: Ocean Waves. CD. Oreade Music, 1999.

Finding God within ourselves & through others

CHAPTER SEVEN

"Secretly we spoke, that wise one and me. I said, 'Tell me the secrets of the world.' He said, 'Sh . . . let silence tell you the secrets of the world.'"

—Jalal-Ud-Din Rumi

Finding God within ourselves & through others

The intrapersonal and interpersonal intelligences are closely linked because the more in touch we are with our own inner motivations and feelings, the more we are able to understand the motivations and feelings of others. The two intelligences are interdependent, each building on the understanding and strengths of the other.

The intrapersonal learners seek to understand their inner worlds. Questions about motivation, feelings, values, integrity, personal strengths, and weaknesses are central to their understanding of themselves and the world around them. Self-knowledge is extremely important to these learners, and they seek quiet time for the reflection needed to acquire this knowledge.

Many of our traditional methods of prayer are designed for the intrapersonal pray-er. Meditation, journaling, contemplative prayer, the examination of conscience, and observing long periods of silence all facilitate the inner life of the intrapersonal learner. All of these techniques can lead to a deeper knowledge of self, an understanding of personal motivations, and the need for personal goal development.

This inner world is, of course, central to the spiritual development of every human being. However, some come to know this inner world better through personal reflection and opportunities for quiet introspection, while others acquire this knowledge through interaction within a supportive group or community.

The interpersonal learners turn outward more often than inward for self-knowledge. The desire to know oneself is equally as strong for the interpersonal pray-er, but the means of acquiring that knowledge are very different. Interaction with others leads to key insights about personal motivation and accountability. These learners have the capacity to understand and interact effectively with others. They can maintain multiple perspectives about an idea or issue and come to know themselves and their own motivations through dialogue and sharing with others. They are sensitive to group dynamics and the feelings of others and have the capacity for self-reflection in group situations.

Opportunities for discussion, journal sharing, and group feedback are important to the interpersonal pray-er. New insights often come through dialogue and the healthy exchange of ideas. Small Christian communities, Bible study groups, and prayer circles provide strong support systems for the interpersonal pray-er.

The qualities of the both the intrapersonal intelligence and the interpersonal intelligence are important for a strong prayer life. They are certainly not mutually exclusive. All of us have within us the need for quiet and the need to interact with others. However, for the intrapersonal pray-er there is a need for greater quiet time and an environment that allows for periods of silence without interruption to come to know God's presence within. The interpersonal pray-er, on the other hand, needs more opportunities to share their insights and reflections with others as a means of deepening his or her relationship with God.

The prayer activities in this chapter are designed to be used two ways—as intrapersonal prayer activities and as interpersonal activities. Individuals and/or groups may choose to use one approach or both. The goal is to deepen our own spirituality by developing a stronger prayer life. There are a number of ways to achieve this objective, but each learner needs to use the method that works best for him or her.

Personal growth sheet

Intrapersonal Prayer: Use this sheet for your own personal prayer and reflection.

Interpersonal Prayer: Do the reflection part by yourself, but find a companion or companions with whom you can share goals as well as the challenges encountered in trying to attain them. Being accountable to and with others can often strengthen your resolution to reach goals.

Describe one goal you would like to achieve this week. (This could be something you hope to accomplish or something you would prefer not to do.)

List specific steps you will take to achieve this goal.

List the challenges you will need to overcome to achieve this goal.

Reflection at the end of the week:

How well did you achieve your goal?

What worked well for you?

What steps can you take to reach future goals?

The story prayer

Throughout history people have passed their wisdom down through the generations by way of stories. Gathered around campfires in every corner of the world, tribal peoples told stories[1] to remind themselves and each other of the wisdom of their people. Jeanette Henry and Rupert Costo, in their book *A Thousand Years of American Indian Storytelling*, tell us that

> *"Storytelling, from ancient times and among all peoples of the earth, had a special role in the life of the people. Storytelling educated the young; it provided entertainment for the grown men and women; it made possible the knowledge of a people's history which was passed on by word of mouth from generation to generation; and it served to teach lessons about how to be good people, with care for others and respect for all of life."*[2]

The wisdom within the following tales can provide glimpses of God's wisdom and vision for the world.

Intrapersonal Prayer: Choose one of the tales below for private prayer. Read it over several times, and allow the words to convey new insights and understandings about life to you. How does the story convey a message of wisdom? How can this story add to your understanding of God's wisdom?

Interpersonal Prayer: Choose one of the stories below to read to and share with a group. Allow each participant to reflect aloud on his or her understanding of the meaning within the story and how that insight can affect his or her life. Each group member can share how God may be revealed through the story.

The Boatman (A Sufi Story from the Middle East)

A scholar asked a boatman to row him across the river. The journey was long and slow. The scholar was bored. "Boatman," he called out, "Let's have a conversation." Suggesting a topic of special interest to himself, he asked, "Have you ever studied phonetics or grammar?"

"No," said the boatman, "I've no use for those tools."

"Too bad," said the scholar, "You've wasted half your life. It's useful to know the rules."

Later, as the rickety boat crashed into a rock in the middle of the river, the boatman turned to the scholar and said, "Pardon my humble mind that to you must seem dim, but, wise man, tell me, have you ever learned to swim?"

"No," said the scholar, "I've never learned. I've immersed myself in thinking."

"In that case," said the boatman, "you've wasted all your life. Alas, the boat is sinking."

A Rock of Birds (A Folktale from India)

There was once a flock of birds peacefully pecking seeds under a tree. A hunter came along and threw a heavy net over them. He said, "Aha! Now I have my dinner."

All at once the birds began to flap their wings. Up, up they rose into the air, taking the net with them. They came down on the tree and, as the net sagged in the tree's branches, the birds flew out from under it to freedom.

The hunter looked on in amazement, scratched his head and muttered, "As long as those birds cooperate with one another like that, I'll never be able to capture them! Each one of those birds is so frail, and yet together they can lift the net."

Ten Jugs of Wine (A Tale from Japan)

Ten old men decided to celebrate the new year with a big crock of hot sake wine. Since none of them could provide for all, they agreed to bring one jug of wine for the large heating bowl. On the way to his wine cellar, each old man thought, "My wine is too valuable to share! No one will know. It'll never show. It'll still be fine. I'll bring a jug of water instead of the wine."

And so when they gathered with the jugs they brought, all ten old men poured the contents of their jugs ceremoniously into the big bowl and then looked sheepishly at one another as they heated and poured hot water for all.

The Purse of Gold (A Jewish Folktale)

A beggar found a leather purse that someone had dropped in the marketplace. Opening it, he discovered that it contained 100 pieces of gold. Then he heard a merchant shout. "A reward! A reward to the one who finds my leather purse!"

Being an honest man, the beggar came forward and handed the purse to the merchant saying, "Here is your purse. May I have the reward now?"

"Reward?" scoffed the merchant, greedily counting his gold. "Why the purse I dropped had 200 pieces of gold in it. You've already stolen more than the reward! Go away or I'll tell the police."

"I'm an honest man," said the beggar defiantly. "Let us take this matter to the court."

In court the judge patiently listened to both sides of the story and said, "I believe you both. Justice is possible! Merchant, you stated that the purse you lost contained 200 pieces of gold. Well, that's a considerable cost. But, the purse this beggar found had only 100 pieces of gold. Therefore, it couldn't be the one you lost."

And, with that, the judge gave the purse and all the gold to the beggar.

The Talkative Turtle (A Tale from India)

A talkative turtle overheard two hunters say that they were planning to catch turtles the very next day. When the hunters left, the turtle asked two cranes to help him escape. "Beautiful white birds," he said, "if you hold a long stick between your beaks, I'll close my mouth tightly in the middle of it, and then you can fly up and carry me to safety."

"Good idea," said the cranes. "But, for the plan to succeed, you will have to keep your mouth closed tightly on the stick and you must not say a word!" The turtle agreed and, biting on the middle of a stick held in the beaks of two birds, off he was carried.

When the birds were in the air with the turtle dangling down from the stick, some people on the ground looked up at the strange sight in the sky and said, "What clever birds! They figured out how to carry a turtle!"

The proud, talkative turtle cried out, "It was my idea!" and fell tumbling down to earth.

[1]All stories used in this section are retold by Heather Forest and reprinted with permission from Story Arts Online http://www.storyarts.org
[2]Henry, Jeanette and Rupert Costo. *A Thousand Years of American Indian Storytelling*. The Indian Historian Press, Inc., 1981. p vii (quoted in Fox, Matthew. *One River, Many Wells*. J.P. Tarcher/Putnam, a member of Penguin Putnam Inc., 2000. p 223.

Collaborative prayer

"I can't be found in myself. I discover myself in others. That much is clear.
And I suspect that I also love and care for myself in others."

—Hugh Prather

In order to meet the needs of both the intrapersonal pray-er and the interpersonal pray-er, this prayer has several parts. The first part allows time for personal quiet and reflection. The second part invites participants to share their personal reflections with others.

Collaboration implies working together. The collaborative prayer extends this idea to praying together. To collaborate in prayer is to open oneself to the insights of others in a shared prayer experience. This prayer can take many forms. There is no one best way to do it. The most important characteristic is the willingness to be open to the voice of the Holy Spirit in one's own life and in the lives of others.

Prayer: Choose one of the following to use in a group setting:

A passage from the Old or New Testament

- All receive a copy of the passage and read it in silence, or the passage is read aloud.
- Allow 5 to 10 minutes for personal reflection on the passage.
- Allow each group member time to share personal insights about the passage.
- Conclude with prayer, either spontaneous or formulaic.

Choose a New Testament story, and divide it into parts so each participant receives only two or three sentences.

- Each group member has the opportunity to read the passage received quietly.
- The group comes together and shares the insights gleaned from the sentences each has read.
- Conclude with prayer together, either spontaneous or formulaic.

Choose a spiritual reading book that all members of the group read ahead of time.

• Each member comes to the group prayer prepared to share his or her understanding of the book's message and how it can be used to deepen his or her Christian life.
• Group members choose a specific action from the discussion that they agree to try to practice during the coming week.
• Conclude with a prayer, either spontaneous or formulaic.

The point-of-view prayer

"If the doors of perception were cleansed, everything would be seen as it is: infinite."
—William Blake

"We see things not as they are, but as we are." This quote (author unknown), surfaces frequently in discussions on perception. Our personal worldview is sometimes the biggest stumbling block to prayer. It can prevent us from looking beyond our immediate experience. It can keep God locked up in a very small box and and confine our imagination to our own little corner of the world. Richard Rohr tells us

> *"I think Christianity has created a great problem in the Western world by repeatedly presenting itself, not as a way of seeing all things, but as one competing ideology among many. Instead of leading us to see God in new and surprising places, it too often has led us to confine God inside our place . . . Prayer is not 'one of the ten thousand things.' It's that by which we see the ten thousand things.... In prayer we see all things in a new light."*[1]

This prayer invites us outside our comfort zones. It beckons us to step into another's shoes to discover God in new and surprising ways. While there are certainly some ideas in non-Christian texts that conflict with Christian doctrine, an open-hearted exploration of other religious traditions can stretch our imaginations and hint at the breadth and persistence of God's call to human persons across cultures. The following writings from a variety of traditions and authors, outside the Judeo-Christian tradition, can reveal new and wondrous surprises about the God who is in all and with all.

Intrapersonal Prayer: Choose any of the following passages to read and reflect on the image(s) of God that emerge. Is this an image of God with which you are familiar? Is it a new and surprising image? What has God chosen to reveal to you about the Divine through this reading?

Interpersonal Prayer: Choose any of the following passages, and share with others the insights you have gained about God. How has God chosen to reveal the Divine to you? How has God chosen to reveal the Divine to others? How does this prayer lead you to a deeper understanding of the God within each human being?

Readings from the Buddhist Tradition

Buddhist Beatitudes

Not to serve the foolish, but to serve the wise;
To honor those worthy of honor—this is the greatest blessing.

Much insight and education, self control and pleasant speech,
And whatever word be well spoken—this is the greatest blessing.

To live righteously, to give help to kindred,
To follow a peaceful calling—this is the greatest blessing.

To be long suffering and meek, to abhor and cease
from evil, Not to be weary in well doing—this is the greatest blessing.

To be gentle, to be patient under reproof,
To be charitable, act virtuously—this is the greatest blessing.

Reverence and humility, contentment and gratitude,
To be pure, to be temperate—this is the greatest blessing.

To dwell in a pleasant land with right desires in the heart,
To bear the remembrance of good deeds—this is the greatest blessing.

Beneath the stroke of life's changes, the mind that shaketh not,
Without grief or passion—this is the greatest blessing.

On every side are invincible they who do acts like these,
On every side they walk in safety—and theirs is the greatest blessing.

"Now may every living thing feeble or strong, omitting none, tall or middle, aged or short, supple or gross of form, seen or unseen, dwelling near or far, born or yet unborn, may every living thing be full of bliss."

—The Buddha

Readings from the Islamic Tradition

He it is [Allah] Who sent down tranquility into the hearts of the believers that they might add faith to their faith—and to Allah belong the hosts of the heavens and the earth, and Allah is All-Knowing, Wise—

—The Holy Qur'an Ch. 48: 5

True believers are only those whose hearts tremble when the name of Allah is mentioned, and who, when His Signs are recited to them, have their faith increased thereby, and who put their trust in their Lord, Who observe Prayer and spend out of that which We have provided for them, These it is who are true believers. They have grades of rank with their Lord, as well as forgiveness and an honourable provision.

—The Holy Qur'an Ch 8: 3–5

O ye who believe! Be steadfast in the cause of Allah, bearing witness in equity; and let not a people's enmity incite you to act otherwise than with justice. Be always just, that is nearer to righteousness. And fear Allah. Surely, Allah is aware of what you do.

—The Holy Qur'an Ch. 5: 9

Readings from the Hindu Tradition

May there be peace in the higher regions; may there be peace in the firmament; may there be peace on earth. May the waters flow peacefully; may the herbs and plants grow peacefully; may all the living powers bring unto us peace. The supreme Lord is peace. May we all be in peace, and only peace; and may that peace come unto each of us.

—The Vedas

I will behold the Invisible in the visible forms of my father, mother and friends, sent here to love and help me. I will show my love for God by loving them all. In their human expressions of affection, I will recognize only the One Divine Love.

—Paramahansa Yogananda

Readings from the Sikh Tradition

In the company of saints and holy people
Yours and mine are no more
Only Thine, O Lord.
No one an enemy, none a stranger
As friends we get on with each other.
What the Lord wills is good.
This wisdom is received in blessing from saints
The One Lord is with us all.

—Adi Granth

May the kingdom of justice prevail!
May the believers be united in love!
May the hearts of the believers be humble, high their wisdom, And may they be guided in their wisdom by the Lord.

"Glory be to God!"
Entrust unto the Lord what thou wishest to be accomplished..
The Lord will bring all matters to fulfillment:
Know this as truth evidenced by Himself.

—A Sikh Prayer

Readings from the Native American Tradition

Let us know peace, for as long as the moon shall rise, for as long as the grass shall grow. Let us know peace.

—Native American Prayer

Earth Prayer
(Ancient Indian Prayer)

To the Great Spirit, give us hearts to understand;
Never to take from creation's beauty more than we give;
Never to destroy wantonly for the furtherance of greed;
Never to deny to give our hands for the building of earth's beauty;

Never to take from her what we cannot use.

Give us hearts to understand
That to destroy earth's music is to create confusion;
That to wreck her appearance is to blind us to beauty;
That to callously pollute her fragrance is to make a house of stench;

That as we care for her she will care for us.

We have forgotten who we are.
We have sought only our own security.
We have exploited simply for our own ends.
We have distorted our knowledge.
We have abused our power.

Great Spirit, whose dry lands thirst,
Help us to find the way to refresh your lands.

Great Spirit, whose waters are choked with debris and
pollution, Help us to find the way to cleanse your waters.

Great Spirit whose beautiful earth grows ugly with misuse,
Help us to find the way to restore beauty in your
handiwork.

Great Spirit, whose creatures are being destroyed,
Help us to find a way to replenish them.

Great Spirit, whose gifts to us are being lost in selfishness
and corruption,
Help us to find the way to restore our humanity.

Oh, Great Spirit, whose voice I hear in the wind, whose
breath gives life top the world, hear me;
I need your strength and wisdom.

May I walk in Beauty.

---

[1] Rohr, Richard. *Everything Belongs*. Crossroad, 1999.

The fable prayer

Aesop's fables[1] have entertained people throughout the ages. These simple tales, which end with morals, challenge us and cause us to think; each one is unique, yet each one reveals a universal principle. The morals in Aesop's fables are as applicable to our times as they were centuries ago. Some of the truths can even be interpreted as being consistent with the universal truths of the Bible.

Intrapersonal Prayer: Choose one of the fables below for personal reflection. Ask yourself what the moral of the story is and what it means in your own life. What universal truth does the moral make you think of? What is God saying to you through this truth?

Interpersonal Prayer: Choose one of the following fables to share with a group. Together, discuss the moral of the story and how it affects your own life. Identify at least one Bible story that is similar or that carries a similar message. What is God saying to you through this truth?

Keeping the Gold

There was once a man who loved gold so much that he melted down all the gold he owned into a huge golden boulder. Thinking that the gold would be easier to keep in this form, he buried the boulder in the ground behind his house. Each night he dug it up, looked at it, and then buried it again.

One night a thief, who had watched the man's nightly task, stole the golden boulder and buried an ordinary stone in its place.

When the man came out to dig up his gold, he discovered the switch and began to moan and shout about his loss. The thief, watching in the shadows, heard the pitiful moans and said, "Why are you so upset? The golden boulder you buried might as well have been stone, for you never, ever used it while you kept it for your own!"

The Pitcher and the Crow

There once was a crow who was terribly thirsty. He noticed a bit of water at the bottom of a tall clay pitcher, but his beak was too wide and the pitcher too thin to poke his thirsty tongue down in.

"What shall I do?" thought the crow. "I'll think and think! I must get myself a drink!"

"Ah HA!" exclaimed the crow as an idea came to him.

He took a pebble in his beak and dropped it over the pitcher's brim. Plop! Plop! He dropped two more in. On and on he went. One by one the pebbles fell, slowly making the water rise until it was easily within reach of his thirsty tongue.

"AHHHH!" he said as he took a drink, "No problem's too big when I think and think."

You Are Beautiful As You Are

There once was a crow who did not like his feathers. "I wish I were a peacock!" he would say.

"You are beautiful as you are!" the other crows insisted.

"How plain and dull you seem to me!" he'd complain, and fly off to admire the peacocks.

The peacocks strutted about with their colorful tail feathers outstretched. To the delight of the crow, some of the peacock feathers fell to the ground when the peacocks left.

Crow flew down to the ground and stuck the peacock feathers into his wings and tail. He attached a few sticking up from his head.

"Now I am as beautiful as a peacock!" he said.

But when he tried to join the peacocks in their strutting, they poked and pecked at him.
What a fuss!

"You are not a peacock," they said, "Don't imitate us!"

Bruised and dragging some broken peacock feathers in his tail, he returned home.

After all his insults, no one wanted his company!

As he sat alone, the other crows said, "It's foolish to try to be what you're not. Learn to love the feathers you've got!"

Zig-Zag Walk

Under the waves at the bottom of the sea, a mother crab scolded her daughter.

"Why are you scurrying side to side in that ridiculous zig-zag walk of yours? Come forward! Walk straight, like other creatures do!"

"But, mother," squeaked the little crab, "I learned to walk from you! If you want something different from me, change the example I see!"

And with that, the little crab zig-zig-zig-zagged away.

---

[1] All stories used in this section are retold by Heather Forest and reprinted with permission from Story Arts Online http://www.storyarts.org

The ninety-nine most beautiful names for God

From the Muslim Tradition

Real prayer always expands our worldview—it beckons, calls, leads, and sometimes pushes us into new spaces from which to view reality. All religious traditions have names by which they refer to the Divine. In one practice within the Muslim tradition, the pray-er recites and reflects on ninety-nine of the most beautiful names for God.

Intrapersonal Prayer: Choose one of the names for God from the list below, and spend time in silent contemplation about its meaning. How is God revealed through this name? What new insights do you gain when reflecting on this name? What does this name of God call you to be?

Interpersonal Prayer: Each member of a group chooses a name of God that is especially meaningful in his or her own life. Participants share their insights about the name they've chosen and why it is significant to them. Participants are invited to listen respectfully to others' sharing allowing their own vision and understanding of God to expand.

The Fashioner
The Maker
The Creator
The Majestic
The Compeller
The Mighty
The Protector
The Giver of Peace
The Author of Safety
The Holy
The Sovereign
The Merciful
The Compassionate
The All-Hearing
The Dishonorer
The Honorer
The Exalter
The Abaser
The Expander
The Constrictor
The All-Knower
The Judge
The Provider
The Bestower
The Dominant
The Forgiver
The Maintainer
The Preserver
The Most Great
The Sublime
The Appreciative
The All-Forgiving
The Great One
The Patient
The Aware
The Subtle One
The Just
The Judge
The All-Seeing

The Trustee
The Truth
The Witness
The Noble
The Loving
The Wise One
The Awakener
The All-Embracing
The Responsive
The Watchful
The Generous One
The Glorious
The Reckoner
The Noble
The Finder
The Self-Subsisting
The Alive
The Giver of Death
The Giver of Life
The Restorer
The Beginner

The Counter
The Praiseworthy
The Protecting Friend
The Firm One
The Most Strong
The Source of All Goodness
The Most Exalted
The Governor
The Hidden
The Manifest
The Last
The First
The Deferrer
The Forward-Bringer
The Powerful
The Able
The Eternal
The One
The Withholder
The Enricher
The Self-Sufficient

The Gatherer
The Equitable
The Lord of Majesty and Bounty
The Lord of the Kingdom
*The Compassionate**
The Pardoner
The Avenger
The Acceptor of Repentance
*The Patient**
The Guide
The Inheritor
The Everlasting
The Originator
The Guide
The Light
The Profiter
The Distresser[1]

**Although in English the translation for these words is the same and may seem repetitious, in Arabic these are different words.*

[1] Fox, Matthew. *One River, Many Wells*. Jeremy P. Tarcher/Putnam, a member of Penguin Putnam, Inc., 2000.

A few quotes about the "interpersonal" to ponder

"Treat people as if they were what they ought to be and you help them to become what they are capable of being."

—Goethe

"Sometimes our light goes out but is blown into flame by another human being. Each of us owes deepest thanks to those who have rekindled the light."

—Albert Schweitzer

"Each friend represents a world in us, a world possibly not born until they arrive, and it is only by this meeting that a new world is born."

—Anais Nin

"Keep the joy of loving God in your heart and share this joy with all you meet . . ."

—Mother Teresa

"The friend given you by circumstances over which you have no control was God's own gift."

—Frederick Robertson

"Friends are angels who lift us up to our feet when our own wings have trouble remembering how to fly."

—Anonymous

"Never doubt that a small group of thoughtful, committed citizens can change the world; indeed, it's the only thing that ever has."

—Margaret Mead

"We're put on this earth not to see through each other, but to see each other through."

—Anonymous

"There is a tremendous strength that is growing in the world through sharing together, praying together, suffering together, and working together."

—Mother Teresa

"There is one thing stronger than all the armies in the world; and that is an idea whose time has come."

—Victor Hugo

"Life's persistent and most urgent question is "What are you doing for others?"

—Anonymous

"With all things and in all things, we are relatives."

—Sioux Proverb

"Humankind has not woven the web of life. We are but one thread within it. Whatever we do to the web, we do to ourselves. All things are bound together. All things connect."

—Chief Seattle

"We are friends; we must assist each other to bear our burdens."

—Osage Saying

"We are all one child spinning through Mother Sky."

—Shawnee Proverb

"It is within my power either to serve God or not to serve God. Serving him, I add to my own good and the good of the whole world. Not serving him, I forfeit my own good and deprive the world of that good which was in my power to create."

—Leo Tolstoy

"O Great Spirit, who made all races, look kindly upon the whole human family, and take away the arrogance and hatred which separates us from our brothers [and sisters]."

—Cherokee Prayer

" . . . if civilization is to survive, we must cultivate the science of human relationships—the ability of all peoples, of all kinds, to live together and work together in the same world, at peace."

—Franklin Delano Roosevelt

Chapter seven resources

Books

Beversluis, Joel (editor). *A Sourcebook for Earth's Community of Religions.* CoNexus Press and Global Education Associates, 1995.

Fox, Matthew. *One River, Many Wells.* J. P. Tarcher/Putnam, 2000.

Potter, Jean and Marcus Braybrooke. *All in Good Faith: A Resource Book for Multi-faith Prayer.* The World Congress of Faiths, 1997.

Roberts, Elizabeth and Elias Amidon (editors). *Earth Prayers from Around the World.* Harper SanFrancisco, 1991.

______________. *Life Prayers from Around the World.* HarperSanFrancisco, 1996.

Rohr, Richard. *Everything Belongs: The Gift of Contemplative Prayer.* Crossroad, 1999.

Schaef, Anne Wilson. *Native Wisdom for White Minds.* Ballantine, 1995.

Electronic Sources

http://www.storyarts.org

. . . Conclusion praying all ways

There are many definitions of prayer, but definitions cannot touch the heart of prayer, whose essence is relationship. A relationship with God is always dynamic, never static. If this relationship is not growing, it is dying. Prayer cannot be something we do simply because it makes us feel good or because we need something. Authentic prayer grows out of an ongoing relationship with God and is characterized by the full range of human experiences, feelings, and emotions.

Prayer should permeate all that we do. A genuine spirituality is always about integration. Prayer is the factor that facilitates the integration of our spirituality into all that we say and do. It is an ongoing call and response between God and us that moves us toward him. God's call and our response are not single isolated events but an ongoing relationship between people very much in love.

But prayer is more than just part of our personal relationship with God. It is the thread that connects us to all of creation. It moves us beyond what we know into uncharted waters. It beckons us to trust, to allow ourselves to be led, and, oftentimes, to be carried into places not of our own choosing.

This book presents a new way of looking at prayer. Borrowing from the educational theory of multiple intelligences, it suggests multiple activities and ways of praying that reach into the wealth of the human experience. Each suggestion was designed to lead to greater integration and wholeness. Each calls us to find God in new and surprising places and people.

I hope that the prayer suggestions throughout this book will lead you to explore new ways of communing with God in your own life. Be adventuresome! Look for God in unexpected places! Look for God in the ordinary places you frequent daily! God is there—beneath you, above you, around you, and within you. Celebrate our wondrous God through words, art, dance, music—the possibilities are endless because God is infinite!